ADVANCE AGENT PLANNING GUIDE
The Executive Protection Specialist's Guide for Conducting Advance Operations

Duke Speed

◆Trener
International

Published by Trener International LLC

Digital design by Telemachus Press, LLC
www.TelemachusPress.com

Cover Designed by Aaniyah Ahmed/99 Designs

Trener International LLC
www.trenerinternational.com

ISBN: 978-1-945330-22-3 (Paperback)

Library of Congress Control Number: 2016957280

Version: 2019.12.02

DEDICATION

This book is dedicated to the all members of government and private sector executive protection details as well as those whom provide a support role. These dedicated professionals always place the highest value and priority on the lives of those whom they are tasked to protect while placing their own lives at significant risk. I salute you for your steadfast courage, integrity, and professionalism. Semper Fidelis.

ACKNOWLEDGEMENTS

To my amazing wife, Kim Campbell Speed: Thank you for your support and belief in this project. Without your enthusiasm and occasional jab in my ribs, this book may have never made it to publication.

To my late grandfather, Clarence Dudley Tilton: Thank you. I have always admired your quiet humility, work ethic, integrity, and kindness. You have always served as a role model for the person I've aspired to be. You are greatly missed, and I look forward to seeing you in the next life one day.

ABOUT THE AUTHOR

Duke Speed is the Founder and President of Trener International, a service-disabled veteran-owned small business focused on providing learning and development, exercise and role player support, logistical support, and staffing solutions for government, defense, public safety, academia, and private sector organizations. Duke's professional career includes 30 years of U.S. federal government service divided between the Federal Law Enforcement Training Center (FLETC), U.S. Federal Air Marshal Service, Federal Aviation Administration, and the U.S. Marine Corps reconnaissance and special operations community (1979-1999 retired). In addition to federal service employment, he has served as an independent contractor for the U.S. Department of State Diplomatic Security Services in Iraq, Federal Emergency Management Agency during the Katrina and Rita disasters, and the U.S. Navy Anti-Terrorism/Force Protection Training Program. In 2019, Duke provided training for organizations of the U.S. Marine Corps, U.S. Army, U.S. Army National Guard, and several state and municipal-level public safety organizations.

Duke has a Bachelor of Science (Magna Cum Laude) in Criminal Justice from National University. He is certified as a Project Management Professional (PMP®) from the Project Management Institute and a Certified Protection Professional (CPP®) from ASIS International. He serves as a member of the ASIS International Executive Protection Council and is a member of the U.S. Department of State Overseas Security Advisory Council (OSAC), the California Tactical Officers Association (CATO), and the International Security Driver Association (ISDA).

TABLE OF CONTENTS

ADVANCE AGENT PLANNING GUIDE
The Executive Protection Specialist's Guide for Conducting Advance Operations

INTRODUCTION

This Advance Agent Planning Guide was designed and developed to provide executive protection specialists with a user-friendly guide for the planning of executive protection operations and all of the associated advance work.

The definition of a successful executive protection operation is to have the Principal and his/her family and staff conduct their respective mission successfully, maintain their professional and personal credibility and reputation throughout the operation, and return to their original destination safely and without incident.

Proper advance work is the key element in assuring that the above takes place. Arguably, advance operations will determine the ultimate success or failure of any executive protection operation. By design, planning and coordination is comprehensive, extremely detail oriented, and advance agents must be meticulous and thorough in their attention to every aspect of the operation.

In layman's terms, advance planning will begin with the Principal's itinerary (the starting point and all destinations that the Principal will travel). All planning is then reverse-engineered in order to plan the administrative, logistical, and security considerations that lead to each destination in the itinerary.

This guide will serve as a comprehensive planning resource that provides a series of tables/checklists that advance agents and advance team members may use to plan for each element of an executive protection operation.

Advance operations are characterized by three separate phases. The phases include:

- Pre-Advance Phase
- Advance Phase
- Executive Protection Operational Planning Phase

Each of these phases will be detailed as the reader advances through the guide.

PRE-ADVANCE PHASE

The Pre-Advance Phase can best be defined as the planning, liaison, and coordination that will be conducted by the advance agent and advance team members prior to the physical occupation and survey of the routes and venues of the executive protection operation.

The vast majority of pre-advance planning is conducted from the executive protection detail's home base or command post. The pre-advance phase of all executive protection operations will involve comprehensive coordination and liaison with all parties (stakeholders) that are involved in the operation. This coordination will include extensive use of the telephone, email, Internet, and other means of communication.

Additionally, advance agents will review and analyze maps, charts, potential routes, venue blueprints and floor plans, and other resources that are related to the operation. Furthermore, they'll review surveys of routes and venues that may have been completed for past operations.

The main take away with the pre-advance phase is that the advance team will collect as much data as they can before conducting the physical occupation/survey of the routes and venues. The physical survey of routes and venues will be conducted during the Advance Phase. During the advance phase, data that was collected during the pre-advance phase will be validated and/or modified as necessary.

The advance agent and advance team members should use the following series of tables to assist in advance planning and execution. The tables will serve as a resource for the development of organizational standard operating procedures (SOPs) and provide a comprehensive, consistent, user-friendly format for collecting data.

Select the tables that are relevant to the executive protection operation and thoroughly complete them by recording the respective data. Once the table is completed for a venue, it is a standard best practice to obtain it as a record for future operations at the respective venue. Maintain a journal/binder of all advance work and related surveys.

ADVANCE AGENT
AND THE ADVANCE TEAM

Pre-Advance Phase: Use the below table to record data about the personnel whom will be assigned to the advance team. The table will provide a record of who participated in the advance planning and their respective role and duties.

ADVANCE AGENT AND THE ADVANCE TEAM		
□ Date Pre-Advance Commenced:	Location of Pre-Advance: □ Home Base/Command Post □ Venue □ Other	
□ Street Address:		
□ City:	□ State:	□ Zip Code:
□ Agent Legal Name & Nickname:	□ Role/Detail Position:	
□ Mobile Tel #:	□ Email Address:	
□ Agent Call Sign:	□ Blood Type:	
□ Allergies: □ N/A	□ Medications: □ N/A	□ Medical Issues: □ N/A

□ Agent Legal Name & Nickname:		□ Role/Detail Position:	
□ Mobile Tel #:		□ Email Address:	
□ Agent Call Sign:		□ Blood Type:	
□ Allergies: □ N/A	□ Medications: □ N/A		□ Medical Issues: □ N/A
□ Agent Legal Name & Nickname:		□ Role/Detail Position:	
□ Mobile Tel #:		□ Email Address:	
□ Agent Call Sign:		□ Blood Type:	
□ Allergies: □ N/A	□ Medications: □ N/A		□ Medical Issues: □ N/A
□ Agent Legal Name & Nickname:		□ Role/Detail Position:	
□ Mobile Tel #:		□ Email Address:	
□ Agent Call Sign:		□ Blood Type:	
□ Allergies □ N/A	□ Medications: □ N/A		□ Medical Issues: □ N/A

EXECUTIVE PROTECTION DETAIL MEMBERS

Pre-Advance Phase: Use the below table to assign executive protection personnel into their *potential* role and duties in the executive protection operation. The advance agent and the advance team members may *pen in* the agents for their respective role in the executive protection operation.

Advance Phase: Final agent assignments will be determined after the physical advance work is completed. Assignments that were *penned in* during the pre-advance phase may change based on the data that is validated and/or modified during the advance phase. Ultimately, the executive protection detail leadership will determine final agent assignments and responsibilities as the final operational plan details are finalized.

EXECUTIVE PROTECTION DETAIL MEMBERS		
☐ Agent Legal Name & Nickname:	☐ Role/Detail Position:	
☐ Mobile Tel #:	☐ Email Address:	
☐ Agent Call Sign:	☐ Blood Type:	
☐ Allergies ☐ N/A	☐ Medications: ☐ N/A	☐ Medical Issues: ☐ N/A

□ Agent Legal Name & Nickname:		□ Role/Detail Position:
□ Mobile Tel #:		□ Email Address:
□ Agent Call Sign:		□ Blood Type:
□ Allergies □ N/A	□ Medications: □ N/A	□ Medical Issues: □ N/A
□ Agent Legal Name & Nickname:		□ Role/Detail Position:
□ Mobile Tel #:		□ Email Address:
□ Agent Call Sign:		□ Blood Type:
□ Allergies □ N/A	□ Medications: □ N/A	□ Medical Issues: □ N/A
□ Agent Legal Name & Nickname:		□ Role/Detail Position:
□ Mobile Tel #:		□ Email Address:
□ Agent Call Sign:		□ Blood Type:
□ Allergies □ N/A	□ Medications: □ N/A	□ Medical Issues: □ N/A
□ Agent Legal Name & Nickname:		□ Role/Detail Position:
□ Mobile Tel #:		□ Email Address:

□ Agent Call Sign:		□ Blood Type:	
□ Allergies □ N/A	□ Medications: □ N/A		□ Medical Issues: □ N/A
□ Agent Legal Name & Nickname:		□ Role/Detail Position:	
□ Mobile Tel #:		□ Email Address:	
□ Agent Call Sign:		□ Blood Type:	
□ Allergies: □ N/A	□ Medications: □ N/A		□ Medical Issues: □ N/A
□ Agent Legal Name & Nickname:		□ Role/Detail Position:	
□ Mobile Tel #:		□ Email Address:	
□ Agent Call Sign:		□ Blood Type:	
□ Allergies □ N/A	□ Medications: □ N/A		□ Medical Issues: □ N/A

PRINCIPAL DATA

Pre-Advance Phase: Use the below table to collect data about the Principal whom the executive protection detail is tasked to safeguard.

The information to be collected about the Principal is comprehensive and very thorough. Although much of the data is very sensitive in nature, every attempt should be made to obtain the information as it will greatly assist the advance agent and fellow team members in the planning of the administrative, logistical, and security considerations of the executive protection operation.

All data related to the Principal should be safeguarded by the executive protection detail and should not be shared with anyone unless they have an operationally-related genuine need to know.

Advance Phase: By design, the data collected about the Principal during the pre-advance phase is very comprehensive and thorough. Upon completion of the advance phase (*the advance agents physically occupying the venue*), the advance agent and team may determine that additional Principal data may need to be collected. Venues may present unique requirements in themselves and the physical occupation of venues by the advance agent team members may point out factors that were not considered during the pre-advance phase. The below table will be updated to reflect the additional considerations.

PRINCIPAL DATA

□ Full Legal Name:

□ Pseudonyms (fictitious names):

□ Nicknames:

□ Call sign to be used during the EP operation:

□ Description (descriptive word picture of the Principal):

□ Photograph: Headshot photo (attached)

□ Photograph: Full-length head-to-foot photograph (attached) that details the profile of the Principal

□ Residential Street Address:

□ City:	□ State:	□ Zip Code:

□ Home Tel #:	□ Mobile Tel #:	□ Pager #:	□ Fax #:

□ Personal Email Address:	□ Alternate Email Address:

□ Map of Neighborhood:	□ Floorplan/Blueprint:

□ Place of Business Street Address:			
□ City:	□ State:		□ Zip Code:
□ Office Tel #:	□ Mobile Tel #:	□ Pager #:	□ Fax #:
□ Primary Official Email Address:		□ Alt. Official Email Address:	
□ Map of Neighborhood:		□ Floorplan/Blueprint:	

Use this section to describe the physical description of the Principal

□ Left Handed / □ Right Handed	□ Height:	□ Weight:
□ Skin Color:	□ Eye Color:	□ Hair Color:

□ Fingerprint card (attached):

□ Tattoos (location on body/size/description). Attach a photograph showing scale and size:
□ None

□ Scars (location on body/size/description). Attach a photograph showing scale and size:
□ None

□ Birth Marks (location on body/size/description). Attach a photograph showing scale and size:
□ None

□ Principal's Interest, Hobbies, Activities, Habits (That Influence Operation):

Use the below section to describe the medical data of the Principal

□ Blood Type:	□ Medical Identification (ID tags/jewelry): □ None

□ Allergies and Treatment: □ None

□ Medications/Prescriptions/Over-the-Counter (type, dosage, and frequency):   □ None

□ Prosthetics (location and type):   □ None

□ Mobility Aids: □ None

□ Medical Conditions/Issues and Treatment: □ None

□ Previous Surgeries and/or Injuries: □ None

□ Dietary/Nutritional Requirements:

□ Primary Care Physician's Name:

□ Street Address:		
□ City:	□ State:	□ Zip Code:
□ Telephone:	□ Email:	
□ Dentist's Name:		
□ Street Address:		
□ City:	□ State:	□ Zip Code:
□ Telephone:	□ Email:	
□ Additional Medical Specialist's Name:		
□ Street Address:		
□ City:	□ State:	□ Zip Code:
□ Telephone:	□ Email:	

Tobacco Use:

□ N/A

□ Cigarettes (brand):

□ Pipe (brand):

□ Chewing (brand):

□ Dip (brand):

□ Immunization Record (international travel):

Use this section to describe known potential threats

☐ Known threats against Principal:

☐ None

☐ Known threats against Principal's family members:

☐ None

☐ Known enemies or organizations that oppose the Principal:

☐ None

☐ Miscellaneous Data:

PRINCIPAL MISCELLANEOUS DATA

The following table is for the recording of data related to long-term Principals. It is used to augment and provide additional data to the previous table. Some of the data may or may not be relevant for the executive protection operation, and its relevance will be decided by the executive protection detail leadership and the best practices and protocols of the executive protection detail.

PRINCIPAL MISCELLANEOUS DATA		
□ Full Legal Name of Spouse/Domestic Partner: □ N/A		
□ Nickname(s):		
□ Call sign to be used during the EP operation (if applicable):		
□ Photograph: Headshot photo (attached): □ Photograph: Full-length head-to-foot photograph (attached) that details the profile of the spouse/domestic partner:		
□ Street Address (Place of Employment):		
□ City:	□ State:	□ Zip Code:

☐ Telephone:	☐ Email Address:

☐ Full Legal Name of Son: ☐ N/A

☐ Nickname(s):

☐ Call sign to be used during the EP operation (if applicable):

☐ Photograph: Headshot photo (attached):   ☐ Photograph: Full-length head-to-foot photograph (attached) that details the profile of the son:

☐ Street Address (University or place of employment):

☐ **City:**	☐ State:	☐ **Zip Code:**

☐ Telephone:	☐ Email Address:

☐ Full Legal Name of Son: ☐ N/A

☐ Nickname(s):

☐ Call sign to be used during the EP operation (if applicable):

☐ Photograph: Headshot photo (attached)   ☐ Photograph: Full-length head-to-foot photograph (attached) that details the profile of the son

☐ Street Address (University or place of employment):

□ City:	□ State:	□ Zip Code:

□Telephone:	□ Email Address:

| □ Full Legal Name of Daughter: |
| □ N/A |

| □ Nickname(s): |

| □ Call sign to be used during the EP operation (if applicable): |

| □ Photograph: Headshot photo (attached):

□ Photograph: Full-length head-to-foot photograph (attached) that details the profile of the daughter: |

| □ Street Address (University or place of employment): |

□ City:	□ State:	□ Zip Code:

□ Telephone:	□ Email Address:

| □ Full Legal Name of Daughter: |
| □ N/A |

| □ Nickname(s): |

| □ Call sign to be used during the EP operation (if applicable): |

| □ Photograph: Headshot photo (attached):

□ Photograph: Full-length head-to-foot photograph (attached) that details the profile of the daughter: |

□ Street Address (University or place of employment):		
□ City:	□ State:	□ Zip Code:
□ Telephone:	□ Email Address:	
□ Principal's Co-Worker (primary point of contact):		
□ Telephone:	□ Email:	
□ Minor-age children route to and from school:		
□ Special needs of children (if any):		
□ Principal's privately owned vehicles (year, make, model, color, license tag #, VIN)		
□ Recreational vehicles (year, make, model, color, registration #): □ Location:		
□ Civic and organizational activities of Principal and spouse/domestic partner:		
Firearms owned by Principal		
□ Make/Model:	□ Serial #:	□ Storage/Security:
□ Make/Model:	□ Serial #:	□ Storage/Security:

□ Make/Model:	□ Serial #:	□ Storage/Security:
□ Make/Model:	□ Serial #:	□ Storage/Security:
□ Make/Model:	□ Serial #:	□ Storage/Security:
□ Make/Model:	□ Serial #:	□ Storage/Security:
□ Make/Model:	□ Serial #:	□ Storage/Security:

□ Credit card information, including names, account numbers, 24-hr phone numbers:
□ Bank account information, including names, account numbers, and phone numbers:
□ Audio or video Recording of Principal's voice:
□ Handwriting sample, including signature:
□ U.S. Passport information (scanned color copy):
□ Diplomatic passport information, if applicable (scanned color copy):
□ Visa information (scanned color copy):
□ Miscellaneous Data:

PRINCIPAL'S ITINERARY

The Principal's itinerary must be known in order to properly plan all of the logistical and security considerations of an executive protection operation.

This Principal's itinerary is organized so that each destination is considered a venue, including enroute travel destinations (i.e. airports, etc). Although an airport is an enroute destination that will lead to a follow-on destination in the Principal's itinerary, it is considered a venue in itself as administrative, logistical, and security considerations must be planned at the enroute destination just like any other venue.

For example, the movement from the Principal's residence to the airport will be planned by the Advance Agent and advance team members with the Principal's residence being the first venue (Point A) and the airport being the second venue (Point B). The itinerary planning should begin with a high-level sketch of each destination in the Principal's itinerary, using the example on the below table.

PRINCIPAL'S ITINERARY

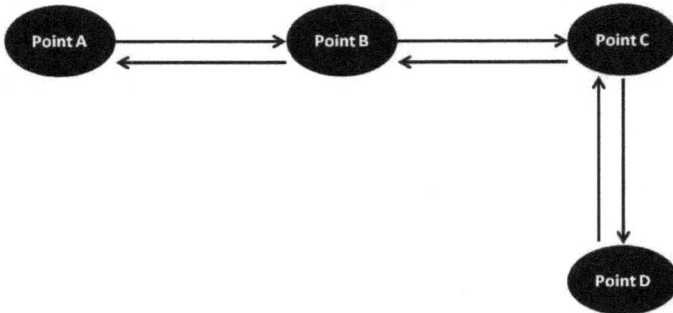

Point A: Principal's Residence
Point B: Los Angeles Airport
Point C: Marriott Hotel
Point D: Smith and Jones Metal Fabrication, LLC (*notional*)
Point C: Marriott Hotel
Point B: Los Angeles Airport
Point A: Principal's Residence

Sketch of Principal's Itinerary (What is the Big Picture?)

Point A:

Point B:

Point C:

Point D:

Point E:

Point F:

Point G:

Point H:

Point I:

Point J:

Sketch the Itinerary Below (Like the above example):

AGENT EQUIPMENT

Pre-Advance Phase: Use the below table for planning the equipment that each detail member will need for the executive protection operation. This section is for *individual* agent equipment planning. Equipment that is specific to *detail/team* equipment will be outlined in later sections of this guide.

Advance Phase: Upon the physical occupation of routes and venues during the advance phase, additional equipment requirements may be determined. The table will be updated to reflect the equipment requirements.

AGENT EQUIPMENT		
Handgun Equipment:		
□ Agent Name:		
□ Handgun Make/Model:	□ Serial Number:	□ Cleaning Kit:
□ Qty./Magazines:	□ Qty./Ammunition:	□ Ammo Make/Model:
□ Miscellaneous Equipment:		

□ Agent Name:		
□ Handgun Make/Model:	□ Serial Number:	□ Cleaning Kit:
□ Qty./Magazines:	□ Qty./Ammunition:	□ Ammo Make/Model:
□ Miscellaneous Equipment:		
□ Agent Name:		
□ Handgun Make/Model:	□ Serial Number:	□ Cleaning Kit:
□ Qty./Magazines:	□ Qty./Ammunition:	□ Ammo Make/Model:
□ Miscellaneous Equipment:		
□ Agent Name:		
□ Handgun Make/Model:	□ Serial Number:	□ Cleaning Kit:
□ Qty./Magazines:	□ Qty./Ammunition:	□ Ammo Make/Model:
□ Miscellaneous Equipment:		
□ Agent Name:		
□ Handgun Make/Model:	□ Serial Number:	□ Cleaning Kit:

□ Qty./Magazines:	□ Qty./Ammunition:	□ Ammo Make/Model:

□ Miscellaneous Equipment:

□ Agent Name:

□ Handgun Make/Model:	□ Serial Number:	□ Cleaning Kit:
□ Qty./Magazines:	□ Qty./Ammunition:	□ Ammo Make/Model:

□ Miscellaneous Equipment:

□ Agent Name:

□ Handgun Make/Model:	□ Serial Number:	□ Cleaning Kit:
□ Qty./Magazines:	□ Qty./Ammunition:	□ Ammo Make/Model:

□ Miscellaneous Equipment:

Rifle/Carbine Equipment:

□ Agent Name:

□ Rifle Make/Model:	□ Serial Number:	□ Cleaning Kit:
□ Qty./Magazines:	□ Qty./Ammunition:	□ Ammo Make/Model:

□ Optics:	□ Miscellaneous Equipment:	
□ Agent Name:		
□ Rifle Make/Model:	□ Serial Number:	□ Cleaning Kit:
□ Qty./Magazines:	□ Qty./Ammunition:	□ Ammo Make/Model:
□ Optics:	□ Miscellaneous Equipment:	
□ Agent Name:		
□ Rifle Make/Model:	□ Serial Number:	□ Cleaning Kit:
□ Qty./Magazines:	□ Qty./Ammunition:	□ Ammo Make/Model:
□ Optics:	□ Miscellaneous Equipment:	
□ Agent Name:		
□ Rifle Make/Model:	□ Serial Number:	□ Cleaning Kit:
□ Qty./Magazines:	□ Qty./Ammunition:	□ Ammo Make/Model:
□ Optics:	□ Miscellaneous Equipment:	
□ Agent Name:		
□ Rifle Make/Model:	□ Serial Number:	□ Cleaning Kit:
□ Qty./Magazines:	□ Qty./Ammunition:	□ Ammo Make/Model:

□ Optics:	□ Miscellaneous Equipment:	
□ Agent Name:		
□ Rifle Make/Model:	□ Serial Number:	□ Cleaning Kit:
□ Qty./Magazines:	□ Qty./Ammunition:	□ Ammo Make/Model:
□ Optics:	□ Miscellaneous Equipment:	
□ Agent Name:		
□ Rifle Make/Model:	□ Serial Number:	□ Cleaning Kit:
□ Qty./Magazines:	□ Qty./Ammunition:	□ Ammo Make/Model:
□ Optics:	□ Miscellaneous Equipment:	

Submachine Gun Equipment:

□ Agent Name:		
□ Submachine Gun Make/Model:	□ Serial Number:	□ Cleaning Kit:
□ Qty./Magazines:	□ Qty./Ammunition:	□ Ammo Make/Model:
□ Optics:	□ Miscellaneous Equipment:	
□ Agent Name:		

□ Submachine Gun Make/Model:	□ Serial Number:	□ Cleaning Kit:
□ Qty./Magazines:	□ Qty./Ammunition:	□ Ammo Make/Model:
□ Optics:	□ Miscellaneous Equipment:	

□ Agent Name:		
□ Submachine Gun Make/Model:	□ Serial Number:	□ Cleaning Kit:
□ Qty./Magazines:	□ Qty./Ammunition:	□ Ammo Make/Model:
□ Optics:	□ Miscellaneous Equipment:	

□ Agent Name:		
□ Submachine Gun Make/Model:	□ Serial Number:	□ Cleaning Kit:
□ Qty./Magazines:	□ Qty./Ammunition:	□ Ammo Make/Model:
□ Optics:	□ Miscellaneous Equipment:	

□ Agent Name:		
□ Submachine Gun Make/Model:	□ Serial Number:	□ Cleaning Kit:
□ Qty./Magazines:	□ Qty./Ammunition:	□ Ammo Make/Model:

□ Optics:	□ Miscellaneous Equipment:	
□ Agent Name:		
□ Submachine Gun Make/Model:	□ Serial Number:	□ Cleaning Kit:
□ Qty./Magazines:	□ Qty./Ammunition:	□ Ammo Make/Model:
□ Optics:	□ Miscellaneous Equipment:	
□ Agent Name:		
□ Submachine Gun Make/Model:	□ Serial Number:	□ Cleaning Kit:
□ Qty./Magazines:	□ Qty./Ammunition:	□ Ammo Make/Model:
□ Optics:	□ Miscellaneous Equipment:	

Additional Agent Equipment:

□ Additional Firearms/Weapons:	□ Additional Ammunition:
□ Concealment Holster:	□ Gun Locks/Cables:
□ Firearm Slings:	□ Multi-Tool/Tactical Folder:
□ Tactical Flashlight/Batteries:	□ Handcuffs/Key/Flex Cuffs:
□ Baton:	□ Body Armor:

□ Agent Individual First-Aid Kit (IFAK):	□ Wrist Watch:
□ Prescription Eyeglasses:	□ Contact Lenses/Solution:
□ Wraparound Glasses (tinted/non-mirror):	□ Wraparound Glasses (clear):
□ Handheld Radio Communication:	□ Radio Batteries:
□ Radio Charger:	□ Surveillance Kit w/Ear Buds:
□ Blue Force Tracker/Agent Beacon Device:	□ Miscellaneous Communication Equipment:
□ Cellular Telephone:	□ Cell Phone Charger:
□ Electrical Power Converter (OCONUS):	□ Alarm Clock:
□ Compass (hand held):	□ Global Positioning System (hand held):
□ Credentials/ID Card/ Badge/Lanyard:	□ Common Access Card:
□ Diplomatic Passport:	□ Tourist Passport:
□ Agency Credit Card/PIN:	□ Personal Credit Card/PIN:
□ U.S. Currency:	□ Local Currency (OCONUS):
□ International Telephone Card:	□ Traveler's Checks:

□ International Driver License:	□ U.S. Driver License:
□ Medical Prescriptions:	
□ Immunization Record:	
□ Detail Attire/Footwear:	□ Civilian Attire/Footwear:
□ Physical Training Attire/Footwear:	□ Cold/Wet Weather Parka:
□ Photojournalist Vest:	□ Overnight Bag/Shaving Kit/Toiletries:
□ Note Pad and Writing Utensil(s):	□ Regional Maps/Charts:
□ Local Language Guide:	□ Planning Checklists:
□ Airline Tickets:	□ Hotel Reservations:
□ Detail SOPs:	□ Miscellaneous Equipment:

DETAIL FIREARMS EQUIPMENT

Pre-Advance Phase: Use the below table to assign additional firearms-related equipment that will be supplemental and additional to the individual agent firearms equipment that was detailed in the previous table.

Advance Phase: Upon the physical occupation of routes and venues during the advance phase, additional firearms-related equipment considerations may be discovered. The table will be updated to reflect the additional equipment considerations.

DETAIL FIREARMS EQUIPMENT		
□ Firearm Make/Model:	□ Serial Number:	□ Cleaning Kit:
□ Firearm Make/Model:	□ Serial Number:	□ Cleaning Kit:
□ Firearm Make/Model:	□ Serial Number:	□ Cleaning Kit:
□ Firearm Make/Model:	□ Serial Number:	□ Cleaning Kit:
□ Firearm Make/Model:	□ Serial Number:	□ Cleaning Kit:

□ Ammo Make/Model:	□ Ammo Quantity:	□ Ammo Caliber:
□ Ammo Make/Model:	□ Ammo Quantity:	□ Ammo Caliber:
□ Ammo Make/Model:	□ Ammo Quantity:	□ Ammo Caliber:
□ Ammo Make/Model:	□ Ammo Quantity:	□ Ammo Caliber:
□ Ammo Make/Model:	□ Ammo Quantity:	□ Ammo Caliber:

□ Concealment Holster: Other Holsters(s):	□ Gun Lock Cables/Gun Boxes:
□ Weapon Optics:	□ Body Armor (for Principal(s):
□ Firearms Range Equipment (for zeroing and proficiency training):	□ Firearms Range Targeting Supplies (targets/staples/pasties/etc.):
□ Eye Protection:	□ Ear Protection:
□ Miscellaneous Equipment:	

COMMAND POST EQUIPMENT

Pre-Advance Phase: Use the below table to outline equipment considerations that may be required for coordinating and establishing the executive protection detail's command post.

Of course, the detail's home-based command post will be well established regarding facilities and equipment. The below table may assist in developing the home base; however, this table will better serve executive protection details when their operation requires the establishment of a mobile command post when they are traveling with their Principal.

The requirements and considerations may vary significantly from operation to operation as the environment will dictate the requirements. Factors such as the geographical location, threat level, and the size and scope of the operation will determine the equipment that will encompass the command post.

Advance Phase: Once the advance agent and team members physically occupy the proposed command post, additional equipment requirements may be discovered. The table will be updated to reflect the additional equipment considerations.

COMMAND POST EQUIPMENT

□ Detail SOPs:	□ Principal Data:
□ Detail Agent Data:	□ Operational Plan:
□ Maps and Charts of Operational Region:	□ Laptop Computers:
□ Firearm Permits (If applicable):	□ Administrative Supplies:
□ PowerPoint Projector(s):	□ Global Positioning System (GPS) with Regional Software:
□ Blue Force Tracker Equipment:	□ Duress Alarm (Principal's Quarters):

□ Still Photo Camera:	□ Spare Batteries:	□ Charger:
□ Video Camera:	□ Spare Batteries:	□ Charger:
□ Handheld Radios:	□ Spare Batteries:	□ Charger:

□ Radio Repeater Equipment:	□ Surveillance Kits and Ear Buds:
□ Sketch Pads and Writing Utensils:	□ Portable Intrusion Alarm (Principal's Quarters):
□ Flip Chart Easel w/ Paper Pads:	□ Colored Markers:
□ Measure Tape:	□ Measure Wheel:

□ Duct Tape:	□ 550 Parachute Cord:
□ Electrical Tape:	□ Painter Tape:
□ Electrical Extension Cords:	□ Desk Lamps:
□ Insect Repellant:	□ Spare Handcuff Keys/Flex Cuffs:
□ Pre-Packaged Food Rations:	□ Snack Items:
□ Bottled Water:	□ Coffee Maker and Accessories:

AGENT INDIVIDUAL FIRST-AID KIT (IFAK)

Pre-Advance Phase: As a matter of standard operating procedure (SOP), the best practices of many executive protection details includes the requirement that each member carry an Individual First-Aid Kit (IFAK) and be trained in the proper use of its contents.

Use the below table to specify the equipment that should be included in each agent's Individual First-Aid Kit (IFAK).

With respect to training, each agent should be trained in emergency medical first responder skills, at a minimum, and ideally should have training for treating trauma-related injuries. The training should follow the internationally-established model of Tactical Combat Casualty Care (TCCC) and/or Tactical Emergency Casualty Care (TECC). Both of these models place a significant emphasis on treating preventable deaths, to include massive exsanguinating hemorrhage, airway issues, tension pneumothorax, hypothermia, and shock.

The IFAK kit should contain trauma-related items that will assist in treating the preventable death injuries mentioned previously. The detail's medical kit (centralized to the detail) will be covered in a later section of this guide.

Advance Phase: The IFAK is typically a standard operating procedure. Upon the determination of the standard contents, the kit should remain fairly consistent; however, if additional equipment considerations are discovered during the physical occupation of routes and venues, the equipment considerations may be updated to reflect the modifications to the IFAK.

AGENT INDIVIDUAL FIRST-AID KIT (IFAK)

□ Medical Bag (for carrying contents):	□ Tactical Casualty Card *(TCCC or TECC Template)*:
□ Grease Pencil/Marker:	□ Medical Shears:
□ Tourniquet(s):	□ CPR Pocket Mask:
□ Nasopharyngeal Airway:	□ Occlusive Chest Seal (2):
□ Military-Style Cravat/Triangular Bandage:	□ Hemostatic Agents:
□ Emergency Space Blanket:	□ Trauma Bandage(2):
□ Additional Mission-Specific Equipment:	

DETAIL MEDICAL KIT

Pre-Advance Phase: Use the below table to specify equipment and supplies that should be included in the executive protection detail's medical kit. This kit is the common medical equipment that should be carried in accordance with the standard operating procedures of the detail. As a general rule of thumb and common best practice, the kit will be carried in one of the motorcade vehicles, and its location and contents should be known by all members of the detail.

The detail's medical kit will contain many of the items of each agent's IFAK, but its contents will also include additional equipment and supplies for treating trauma and non-trauma injuries and illnesses. The kit should contain enough supplies to cover the scope and span of the executive protection operation.

In the ideal setting, there should be at least one agent trained and certified at the Emergency Medical Technician (EMT) and/or Paramedic level in order to provide advanced life support/medical treatment to casualties, especially in remote or high threat environments.

Advance Phase: During the physical occupation of routes and venues, additional medical equipment and supply considerations may be discovered. Update the table to reflect these additional equipment considerations.

DETAIL MEDICAL KIT	
□ Medical Bag (Marked with Red Cross):	□ Principal's Medical Data Card: □ Agent's Medical Data Card:
□ Litter/Stretcher/Spine Board:	□ Automatic External Defibrillator (AED):
□ Cervical Collar:	□ Sterile Irrigation Water:
□ Nitrile Gloves (Numerous):	□ Medical Shears:
□ Tourniquets:	□ CPR Pocket Mask(s):
□ Nasopharyngeal Airway(s):	□ Bag Valve Mask:
□ Occlusive Chest Seals:	□ Hemostatic Agents:
□ Decompression Needle 14g x 3.25:	□ Military-Style Cravat/Triangular Bandage:
□ Trauma Compression Bandage 6" (2):	□ Abdominal Bandage 12":
□ Elastic Bandage:	□ Oval Eye Dressing(s):
□ Emergency Space Blanket:	□ Burn Dressing(s):
□ Tampons:	□ Chemical Ice Packs:

□ Sam Splints (assorted sizes):	□ Moleskin:
□ Air Splint:	□ Gauze (rolls):
□ Non-Aspirin Pain Reliever:	□ Aspirin:
□ Allergy Medications:	□ Band-Aids (assorted sizes)
□ Antibiotic Ointment:	□ Alcohol Pads:
□ Activated Charcoal:	□ Ammonia Inhalants:
□ Sterile Burn Dressing:	□ Oral Glucose:
□ Oxygen Tank:	□ Duct Tape (rolls):

MOTORCADE EQUIPMENT

Pre-Advance Phase: Use the below table as a checklist of equipment for motorcade movement and its respective motorcade vehicles.

The contents of this equipment table will most likely vary significantly from one operation to the next, depending on the mission profile and several environmental factors related to the geographic location of the operation, the visibility/profile, and the size and scope of the operation.

This table should serve as a general guideline, but it is not all-inclusive. Every detail's standard operating procedures will dictate the motorcade equipment requirements.

Advance Phase: Additional equipment considerations that were discovered during the physical occupation of routes and venues will be added to the table. As mentioned previously, motorcade equipment considerations will vary significantly from one operation to the next with several factors coming into play. These factors include the size and scope of the operations, level of support from external organizations, the threat level, geographic environment, and several other factors.

MOTORCADE EQUIPMENT

Complete the table checklist of equipment for motorcade

Motorcade Vehicle: □ Lead □ Limousine □ Follow □ Other:

□ Vehicle Registration:	□ Vehicle Manufacturer Handbook:
□ Insurance Card:	□ Maps and Charts of Operational Region:
□ Cellular Phone:	□ Cellular Charger:
□ Vehicle Placards:	□ Vehicle Flags:
□ Spare Keys: Maintained: □ Agent-In-Charge □ Driver □ Shift Leader □ Other:	□ Spare Tire (inspected prior to operation): □ Lug Wrench □ Hydraulic and/or Mechanical Jack Kit:
□ Global Positioning System (GPS)with Regional Software:	□ GPS Charger:
□ Hand-Held Compass:	□ Fire Extinguisher:
□ Flares/Safety Cones:	□ Emergency Lights/Siren:
□ Vehicle Radio(s):	□ Radio Charger:	□ Batteries:

□ Jumper Cables	□ Battery Charger Kit:	□ Auto Mechanic's Tool Kit:
□ Sledge Hammer	□ Axe	□ Fix-A-Flat Spray:
□ Crow Bar	□ Tow Chain/Rope:	□ Bolt Cutters:
□ Flashlight w/ Batteries:	□ Spotlight:	□ Spare Fuses:
□ Coveralls:	□ Work Gloves	□ Window Cleaner/Towels:
□ Blankets:	□ Umbrella:	□ Chemical Masks:
□ Hand Cleaner/Towels:	□ Air/Oil Filters:	□ Funnel:
□ Cans of Oil:	□ Fuel Can w/ Gas/Diesel:	□ Chemical Lights
□ VS-17 Panels	□ Shovel	□ Fuel Spill Absorbent:
Body Armor (Supplemental):	□ Back-Up Weapons: □ Ammunition: □ Smoke Grenades: □ Pyrotechnics:	□ Traffic Flares/Cones:
□ Hand Held Magnetometer:	□ Bungee Cords:	□ Tie Downs:
□ Bottled Water:	□ Emergency Food Rations:	

□ Detail Medical Kit (Staged in Designated Motorcade Vehicle):	□ Principal's Bailout Bag (Principal's Limousine):
□ Local Currency (OCONUS):	□ U.S. Currency:
□ Additional Mission-Specific Equipment:	

Complete the table checklist for each motorcade vehicle Motorcade Vehicle: □ Lead □ Limousine □ Follow □ Other:	
□ Vehicle Registration:	□ Vehicle Manufacturer Handbook:
□ Insurance Card:	□ Maps and Charts of Operational Region:
□ Cellular Phone:	□ Cellular Charger:
□ Vehicle Placards:	□ Vehicle Flags:
□ Spare Keys: Maintained: □ Agent-In-Charge □ Driver □ Shift Leader □ Other:	□ Spare Tire (inspected prior to operation): □ Lug Wrench □ Hydraulic and/or Mechanical Jack Kit:
□ Global Positioning System (GPS)with Regional Software:	□ GPS Charger:

□ Hand-Held Compass:	□ Fire Extinguisher:	
□ Flares/Safety Cones:	□ Emergency Lights/Siren:	
□ Vehicle Radio(s):	□ Radio Charger:	□ Batteries:
□ Jumper Cables	□ Battery Charger Kit:	□ Auto Mechanic's Tool Kit:
□ Sledge Hammer	□ Axe	□ Fix-A-Flat Spray:
□ Crow Bar	□ Tow Chain/Rope:	□ Bolt Cutters:
□ Flashlight w/ Batteries:	□ Spotlight:	□ Spare Fuses:
□ Coveralls:	□ Work Gloves	□ Window Cleaner/Towels:
□ Blankets:	□ Umbrella:	□ Chemical Masks:
□ Hand Cleaner/Towels:	□ Air/Oil Filters:	□ Funnel:
□ Cans of Oil:	□ Fuel Can w/ Gas/Diesel:	□ Chemical Lights
□ VS-17 Panels	□ Shovel	□ Fuel Spill Absorbent:
□ Body Armor (Supplemental):	□ Back-Up Weapons: □ Ammunition: □ Smoke Grenades: □ Pyrotechnics:	□ Traffic Flares/Cones:

□ Hand Held Magnetometer:	□ Bungee Cords:	□ Tie Downs:
□ Bottled Water:		□ Emergency Food Rations:
□ Detail Medical Kit (Staged in Designated Motorcade Vehicle):		□ Principal's Bailout Bag (Principal's Limousine):
□ Local Currency (OCONUS):		□ U.S. Currency:
□ Additional Mission-Specific Equipment:		

Complete the table checklist for each motorcade vehicle

Motorcade Vehicle: □ Lead   □ Limousine   □ Follow   □ Other:

□ Vehicle Registration:	□ Vehicle Manufacturer Handbook:
□ Insurance Card:	□ Maps and Charts of Operational Region:
□ Cellular Phone:	□ Cellular Charger:
□ Vehicle Placards:	□ Vehicle Flags:

□ Spare Keys: Maintained: □ Agent-In-Charge □ Driver □ Shift Leader □ Other:	□ Spare Tire (inspected prior to operation): □ Lug Wrench □ Hydraulic and/or Mechanical Jack Kit:
□ Global Positioning System (GPS)with Regional Software:	□ GPS Charger:
□ Hand-Held Compass:	□ Fire Extinguisher:
□ Flares/Safety Cones:	□ Emergency Lights/Siren:

□ Vehicle Radio(s):	□ Radio Charger:	□ Batteries:
□ Jumper Cables	□ Battery Charger Kit:	□ Auto Mechanic's Tool Kit:
□ Sledge Hammer	□ Axe	□ Fix-A-Flat Spray:
□ Crow Bar	□ Tow Chain/Rope:	□ Bolt Cutters:
□ Flashlight w/ Batteries:	□ Spotlight:	□ Spare Fuses:
□ Coveralls:	□ Work Gloves	□ Window Cleaner/Towels:
□ Blankets:	□ Umbrella:	□ Chemical Masks:
□ Hand Cleaner/Towels:	□ Air/Oil Filters:	□ Funnel:

□ Cans of Oil:	□ Fuel Can w/ Gas/Diesel:	□ Chemical Lights
□ VS-17 Panels	□ Shovel	□ Fuel Spill Absorbent:
Body Armor (Supplemental):	□ Back-Up Weapons: □ Ammunition: □ Smoke Grenades: □ Pyrotechnics:	□ Traffic Flares/Cones:
□ Hand Held Magnetometer:	□ Bungee Cords:	□ Tie Downs:

□ Bottled Water:	□ Emergency Food Rations:
□ Detail Medical Kit (Staged in Designated Motorcade Vehicle):	□ Principal's Bailout Bag (Principal's Limousine):
□ Local Currency (OCONUS):	□ U.S. Currency:

□ Additional Mission-Specific Equipment:

Complete the table checklist for each motorcade vehicle

Motorcade Vehicle: □ Lead   □ Limousine   □ Follow   □ Other:

□ Vehicle Registration:	□ Vehicle Manufacturer Handbook:
□ Insurance Card:	□ Maps and Charts of Operational Region:

□ Cellular Phone:	□ Cellular Charger:
□ Vehicle Placards:	□ Vehicle Flags:
□ Spare Keys: Maintained: □ Agent-In-Charge □ Driver □ Shift Leader □ Other:	□ Spare Tire (inspected prior to operation): □ Lug Wrench □ Hydraulic and/or Mechanical Jack Kit:
□ Global Positioning System (GPS)with Regional Software:	□ GPS Charger:
□ Hand-Held Compass:	□ Fire Extinguisher:
□ Flares/Safety Cones:	□ Emergency Lights/Siren:

□ Vehicle Radio(s):	□ Radio Charger:	□ Batteries:
□ Jumper Cables	□ Battery Charger Kit:	□ Auto Mechanic's Tool Kit:
□ Sledge Hammer	□ Axe	□ Fix-A-Flat Spray:
□ Crow Bar	□ Tow Chain/Rope:	□ Bolt Cutters:
□ Flashlight w/ Batteries:	□ Spotlight:	□ Spare Fuses:
□ Coveralls:	□ Work Gloves	□ Window Cleaner/Towels:

□ Blankets:	□ Umbrella:	□ Chemical Masks:
□ Hand Cleaner/Towels:	□ Air/Oil Filters:	□ Funnel:
□ Cans of Oil:	□ Fuel Can w/ Gas/Diesel:	□ Chemical Lights
□ VS-17 Panels	□ Shovel	□ Fuel Spill Absorbent:
Body Armor (Supplemental):	□ Back-Up Weapons: □ Ammunition: □ Smoke Grenades: □ Pyrotechnics:	□ Traffic Flares/Cones:
□ Hand Held Magnetometer:	□ Bungee Cords:	□ Tie Downs:

□ Bottled Water:	□ Emergency Food Rations:
□ Detail Medical Kit (Staged in Designated Motorcade Vehicle):	□ Principal's Bailout Bag (Principal's Limousine):
□ Local Currency (OCONUS):	□ U.S. Currency:
□ Additional Mission-Specific Equipment:	

AGENT BAILOUT BAG EQUIPMENT

Pre-Advance Phase: It is a standard industry best practice that each agent possesses a bailout bag in the unfortunate scenario that involves the executive protection detail and their Principal "ditching" the motorcade vehicles during an attack and/or an escape and evade crisis. It may be due to the motorcade vehicle(s) becoming disabled, blocked, or some other tactical reason. Regardless, this is far from the ideal situation, but should be considered nonetheless.

If the agents and their Principal are without motorcade vehicles, and become dependent on being foot mobile specifically, they are particularly vulnerable to threats, especially in high threat environments.

Of course, this type of scenario involves a worst-case crisis that is more likely to occur in high threat regions outside of the United States, but certainly possible anywhere. Essentially, the equipment should provide each agent with a short-term means of safety, security, and survival during a crisis until a rescue or safe return to base has been achieved.

Executive protection details should develop the standard operating pro-cedures and protocols for the development and use of bailout bags as it relates to their respective mission profile and tactical operational environment.

If determined by the executive protection detail leadership that a bailout bag is developed, it should contain the five main elements of a standard survival kit:

1. Food-gathering equipment/supplies
2. Water-gathering equipment/supplies
3. Shelter-producing equipment/supplies
4. Fire-starting equipment/supplies
5. Signaling equipment/supplies.
6. Additionally, it may contain mission-specific equipment and supplies as it relates to agency standard operating procedures and the respective executive protection operation.

Use the below table to specify equipment that should be included in the individual agent's bailout bag.

Advance Phase: As mentioned previously, an agent bailout bag (if used) is generally a standard operating procedure (SOP) and is fairly consistent from one operation to the next. If additional equipment or supply considerations are discovered during the physical occupation of routes and venues, the table may be updated to reflect the additional considerations.

AGENT BAILOUT BAG EQUIPMENT	
□ U.S. Currency:	□ Local Currency (OCONUS):
□ Rain Jacket:	□ Cold Weather Parka:
□ Emergency Food Rations:	□ Emergency Water Rations:
□ Flint Stone/Waterproof Matches/Lighter:	□ Water Filter or Purifier Tablets:
□ Hand-Held Compass and/or GPS:	□ Spare Socks:

☐ Regional Maps/Charts:	☐ Escape and Evasion Map:
☐ Radio w/ Batteries:	☐ Tactical Flashlight w/ Batteries:
☐ Strobe Light:	☐ Chemical Lights:
☐ 550 Cord (25 Feet):	☐ Duct Tape:
☐ Agent Firearm:	☐ Ammo Magazines/Ammo:
☐ Agent IFAK:	☐ Additional Mission-Specific Equipment:

ROUTE RECONNAISSANCE AND ROUTE SURVEY

Pre-Advance Phase: Use the below table to plan potential routes that will be used during the Principal's itinerary. It is critical that the advance agent/team have a clear understanding of the Principal's itinerary as the route reconnaissance and respective planning is all based on the itinerary.

Movement from one itinerary point to another is considered a route, while directional turns throughout the route are considered legs. Recall the Principal's itinerary sketch that is to be completed by the advance agent team members. This table should be completed for each route (i.e. Point A to Point B, Point B to Point C, etc.)

During the pre-advance phase, the majority of the route reconnaissance and route survey work will be conducted from the executive protection detail's home base/command post through detailed map and chart analysis, use of the Internet, the study of past advances that were conducted of the routes, and various other resources.

Advance Phase: During the advance phase, the team will actually "run the routes", meaning that they will literally drive the planned routes and validate and/or modify the data that was developed during the pre-advance phase. Without question, data will be discovered that was not considered during the pre-advance phase. It will be the responsibility of the advance agent and fellow advance team members to modify the proposed routes as required.

ROUTE RECONNAISSANCE AND ROUTE SURVEY

□ Route from Point _____ to Point _____

□ Route Plan (what is the big picture?):

□ Route (attach map and/or sketch):
□ Note Pertinent Information (key turns/intersections/terrain features):

□ Primary Departure Point:	□ Strong-Side Departure (right) □ Weak-Side Departure (left)
□ Alternate Departure Point:	□ Strong-Side Departure (right) □ Weak-Side Departure (left)
□ Primary Arrival Point:	□ Strong-Side Arrival (right) □ Weak-Side Arrival (left)
□ Alternate Arrival Point:	□ Strong-Side Arrival (right) □ Weak-Side Arrival (left)

□ Weekday Flow of Traffic:
□ Time of Day:_____
□ Light
□ Moderate
□ Heavy
□ Peak Travel Times:_____

Weekend and Holiday/Special Events Flow of Traffic:
□ Time of Day:_____
□ Light
□ Moderate
□ Heavy
□ Peak Travel Times:_____

> □ Road Conditions (paved, gravel, pot holes, etc.):

> *Potential Choke Points (record data below)*

> □ Toll Booths/Procedures/Cost of Tolls:
> □ Word description:
> □ Attach photo and/or video:

> □ Tunnels:
> □ Word description:
> □ Attach photo and/or video:

> □ Bridges/Draw Bridges:
> □ Word description:
> □ Attach photo and/or video:

> □ Railroad/Road Intersections:
> □ Word description:
> □ Attach photo and/or video:

> □ Overpasses:
> □ Word description:
> □ Attach photo and/or video:

> □ Construction Zones:
> □ Word description:
> □ Attach photo and/or video:

□ School/University Zones:

□ Word description:

□ Attach photo and/or video:

□ High Ground/Tall Buildings That Motorcade Will Pass:

□ Word description:

□ Attach photo and/or video:

□ Additional Choke Points:

□ Word description:

□ Attach photo and/or video:

□ Known Special Events/Activities Planned During Principal's Itinerary:

□ Name of Event

□ Word description:

□ Check Points/Phase Lines Location and Description: □ Attach photo and/or video:	□ Radio communication code assigned to check point or phase line:

□ Other Danger Areas/Hazards:

□ Medical Facilities/Type (Along the Route):

□ Designated Safe Havens (Along the Route):

□ Fire/EMS Facilities (Along the Route):

□ Law Enforcement Facilities (Along the Route):

□ Additional Data:

□ **Determine Major Motorcade Legs and Driving Times for Each Leg:**

_____ to _____ Driving Time: ___ Hrs ___ Minutes

_____ to _____ Driving Time: ___ Hrs ___ Minutes

_____ to _____ Driving Time: ___ Hrs ___ Minutes

_____ to _____ Driving Time: ___ Hrs ___ Minutes

_____ to _____ Driving Time: ___ Hrs ___ Minutes

_____ to _____ Driving Time: ___ Hrs ___ Minutes

_____ to _____ Driving Time: ___ Hrs ___ Minutes

_____ to _____ Driving Time: ___ Hrs ___ Minutes

_____ to _____ Driving Time: ___ Hrs ___ Minutes

_____ to _____ Driving Time: ___ Hrs ___ Minutes

SAFE HAVEN SURVEY

Pre-Advance Phase: Use the below table for collecting data related to the planning of potential safe havens. The determination, use, and designation of safe havens are based on the best practices and protocols of executive protection details. Each detail will have its own specific protocol for the use of safe havens. They are most often used in high threat regions or international travel, and may not be used at all during domestic operations.

It is the opinion of the author that safe havens should be identified during all executive protection operations as it is a best practice to prepare for the worst possible scenario, which includes an attack, explosion, fire, and other similar crisis events.

If the executive protection detail decides to plan for the use of safe havens, they should be identified at each of the Principal's venues within his/her itinerary as well as travel between venues throughout each route. A survey should be conducted for every proposed safe haven.

As a general guideline, the advance agent and team members should ask themselves the following questions when considering potential safe havens:
1. Is the safe haven ACCESSIBLE?
2. Is the safe haven SECURE?
3. Do we have the ability to DEFEND the safe haven?
4. Do we have the ability to COMMUNICATE in the safe haven?
5. Do we have the ability to ESCAPE from the safe haven?
6. Do we have the ability to HOLD the safe haven?

Of course, the above six questions are very subjective. They should be answered based on how the executive protection detail defines the six key words that are capitalized. The definition of the six key words will determine the characteristics of the safe haven and assist in their pre-advance planning.

Advance Phase: The data collected during the pre-advance phase will be validated and/or modified during the actual physical occupation of the proposed safe haven during the advance phase.

SAFE HAVEN SURVEY		
□ Date Survey Was Conducted: □ Time of Day: □ Advance Agent:		
□ Name of Venue:		
□ Street Address:		
□ City:	□ State/Country (OCONUS):	□ Zip Code:
□ Description of Venue (attach photo and/or sketch):		
□ Scenario of Venue (what will take place?):		
□ Weather Prediction (date of event):		
□ Primary Point of Contact (POC)/Meet-and-Greet Contact Information:	□ Telephone: □ Alternate Telephone: □ Email:	

On-Site Police/Security:	On-Site Police/Security Personnel:
□ No	Armed: □ Yes □ No
□ Yes (Uniform) Qty. on Duty: __	Arrest Authority: □ Yes □ No
□ Yes (Plain Clothes) Qty. on Duty:__	First-Aid/CPR Trained:
□ Unknown	□ Yes □ No
	Access Master Keys/Card:
	□ Yes □ No
	Access Elevator System:
	□ Yes □ No
	English-Speaking □ Yes □ No

Fire Alarm System:	Sprinkler System:
Local Alarms Only: □ Yes □ No	Water: □ Yes □ No
Site Security Auto Alert:	Foam/Chemical: □ Yes □ No
□ Yes □ No	HALON: □ Yes □ No
Fire Dept Auto Alert: □ Yes □ No	Unknown □
Unknown □	
During Activation:	
□ Strobe	
□ Siren	
□ Horn	
□ Other	

□ Location of Fire Extinguishers:

□ Location of Fire Alarm Pull Stations:

□ Location of Onsite Medical Equipment/AED:

□ Roof Access Procedures:

□ Closed-Circuit Video/Camera: □ No □ Yes – Recorded □ Yes – Not Recorded	□ Location of Monitors and □ Cameras (Attach Photo and/or Sketch):

□ Length of Time that Camera Tapes are Maintained:

Role of Facility Security Personnel:
- □ None
- □ Elevator Access Control
- □ Roving Foot Patrol
- □ Roving Automobile Patrol
- □ Coordination with Law Enforcement
- □Traffic/Parking/Motorcade Security
- □ Security Checkpoints (List Locations)

□ Potable Water	□ Running Water	□ Toilet	□ Shower
□ Medical Support	□ Security Support	□ Commo Support	□ Ingress/Egress

□ Test Cellular Phone and Radio Communications:

□ Physical location of safe haven within venue/address:

□ Instructions for Detail/Agents *(describe how the Principal will be safeguarded and secured)*:

HOSPITAL/MEDICAL FACILITY SURVEY

Pre-Advance Phase: Use the below table to record data for a hospital and medical facility survey. Advance team members will need to plan for and conduct a survey of medical facilities that may be potentially used during the Principal's itinerary.

With any executive protection operation, the advance agent and advance team members must plan for all potential contingencies, including the unfortunate scenario of a medical crisis involving the Principal, a member of the Principal's staff, executive protection detail members, and the general public.

Agency protocols and best practices should specifically address the procedures for handling a medical crisis involving the Principal and detail members. The best practices will determine the executive protection detail's response during an actual medical crisis. Of course, a real world medical crisis will require immediate first responder treatment by the executive protection detail members; however, protocols should dictate that the casualty or casualties receive advanced medical support at a designated medical facility. A medical facility will provide resources that are well beyond the capabilities of first responders within the detail.

Advance Phase: Upon the physical occupation of the hospital/medical facility, additional administrative, logistical, and security considerations may be discovered. The table will be updated to reflect the additional considerations.

HOSPITAL/MEDICAL FACILITY SURVEY

□ Date Survey Was Conducted:

□ Time of Day:

□ Advance Agent:

□ Name of Venue:	Religious Affiliation *(if applicable)*:

□ Street Address:

□ City:	□ State/Country (OCONUS):	□ Zip Code:

□ Description of Venue (attach photo and/or sketch):

□ Scenario of Venue (what will take place?):

□ Weather Prediction (date of event):

□ Primary Point of Contact (POC)/Meet-and-Greet Contact:

□ Primary Point of Contact (POC)/Meet-and-Greet Contact Information:	□ Telephone: □ Alternate Telephone: □ Email:
Facility Type: □ Civilian □ Military	□ In-Patient □ Out-Patient
□ ER Hours (If Not 24 Hour):	□ Walk-In Hours (If Not 24 Hour):
English Spoken at Facility: □ Yes □ No	Interpreter on Duty/Available □ Yes □ No

□ Emergency Room (ER) POC:	□ Telephone:
□ Alternate ER POC:	□ Telephone:
□ Ambulance POC:	□ Telephone:
□ Aviation MEDEVAC POC:	□ Telephone:
□ Security POC:	□ Telephone:
□ Building Engineer POC:	□ Telephone:

□ Closest Medical Facility Name:
□ Street Address:

□ City:	□ State:	□ Zip Code:

□ What Types of Cases are Referred to Other Medical Facilities?
□ Medical Facilities Where Referrals are Sent:
Is There a Protocol to Notify Facility of VIP? □ Yes □ No Describe:
□ What is Protocol for VIP Being Evaluated and/or Admitted?

□ Anesthesiologist	□ Emergency Room	□ Neurosurgeon	□ Radiologist
□ Burn Center	□ General Surgeon	□ Operating Room/Team	□ Thoracic Surgeon
□ Cardiologist	□ Helipad	□ Ophthalmologist	□ Trauma Center

□ Clinical Lab	□ Intensive Care Unit	□ Orthopedic Surgeon	□ Whole Blood
□ Coronary Care Unit	□ Internist	□ Pathologist	□ X-Ray
□ Dental Unit	□ MEDEVAC	□ Pharmacy	□ Other

Helipad Location and Procedures (Grid/Lat/Lon Coordinates):

On-Site Security:

□ No

□ Yes (Uniform)

Qty. on Duty: __

□ Yes (Plain Clothes)

Qty. on Duty:__

□ Unknown

On-Site Security Personnel:

Armed: □ Yes □ No

Arrest Authority: □ Yes □ No

First-Aid/CPR Trained:

□ Yes □ No

Access Master Keys/Card:

□ Yes □ No

Access Elevator System:

□ Yes □ No

English-Speaking □ Yes □ No

Fire Alarm System:

Local Alarms Only: □ Yes □ No

Site Security Auto Alert:

□ Yes □ No

Fire Dept Auto Alert: □ Yes □ No

Unknown □

During Activation:

□ Strobe

□ Siren

□ Horn

□ Other

Sprinkler System:

Water: □ Yes □ No

Foam/Chemical: □ Yes □ No

HALON: □ Yes □ No

Unknown □

□ Location of Fire Extinguishers:

□ Location of Fire Alarm Pull Stations:

□ Highest Floor that Fire Ladder Can Reach (Ideal Locations for Fire Ladder Truck):

Closed-Circuit Video/Camera: □ No □ Yes – Recorded □ Yes – Not Recorded	□ Location of Monitors and Cameras (Attach Photo and/or Sketch):

□ Length of Time that Camera Tapes are Maintained:

Access Control of Elevators: All Floors: □ Yes □ No Some Floors: □ Yes □ No None □	Access Control of Stairwells: All Floors: □ Yes □ No Some Floors: □ Yes □ No None □

Access Control of Garage: Attendant: □ Yes □ No Key/Card: □ Yes □ No None □	Access Control of Roof: Key/Card: □ Yes □ No Location of Access:

Role of Medical Facility Security Personnel During Principal Stay:

□ None

□ Elevator Access Control

□ Roving Foot Patrol

□ Roving Automobile Patrol

□ Coordination with Law Enforcement

□ Traffic/Parking/Motorcade Security

□ Security Checkpoints (list locations):

□ Safe Haven Location/Description/Procedures:

□ Instructions to Detail/Agents:

AIRPORT/AVIATION FACILITY SURVEY

Pre-Advance Phase: Use the below table as a guide for the conduct of an airport or other type of aviation facility survey.

If the Principal's itinerary includes travel via aviation assets, the airport/aviation facility is considered to be a venue. Like any venue in the Principal's itinerary, it must be surveyed and all administrative, logistical, and security considerations must be planned by the advance agent and advance team members.

No two airports are alike and each airport facility is unique in itself. International aviation laws, rules, and regulations vary among nations and domestic and international airports vary significantly in size and scope. There are literally hundreds of administrative, logistical, and security factors that should be included in the survey and it can be a tall order for an advance agent and his/her team.

Advance Phase: Data that was discovered during the pre-advance phase will be validated and/or modified during the physical occupation of the airport/aviation facility. Inevitably, the advance phase will discover data that was not considered during the pre-advance phase. It is the responsibility of the advance agent and fellow advance team members to update the table to reflect the modifications.

AIRPORT/AVIATION FACILITY SURVEY

□ Date Survey Was Conducted:

□ Time of Day:

□ Advance Agent:

□ Name of Venue:	□ Airport Code:

□ Street Address:

□ City:	□ State/Country (OCONUS):	□ Zip Code:
□ Map of Airport:	□ Map of Region:	□ Blueprint/Sketch:

□ Word description of Venue (Attach Photo and/or Sketch):

□ Noteworthy Security Challenges/Problems Encountered:

□ Scenario of Venue (what will take place?):

□ Length of Runway:

□ Largest Aircraft that Can Support a Takeoff and Landing:

□ Takeoff:

□ Landing:

□ Planned Arrival Date:	□ Planned Arrival Time:	□ Planned Departure Date:	□ Planned Departure Time:

□ Weather Prediction (date of event):

□ Primary Point of Contact (POC)/Meet-and-Greet Contact:	
□ Primary Point of Contact (POC)/ □ Meet-and-Greet Contact Information:	□ Telephone: □ Alternate Telephone: □ Email:
□ Hotel Reservations (If Applicable):	
□ Airline Reservations (If Applicable):	
□ Airport Operating Hours: □ 24 Hr □ Other:	□ TARMAC Accessible: □ 24 Hr □ Other
English Spoken at Facility: □ Yes □ No	Interpreter on duty/Available: □ Yes □ No
Type of Airport (Domestic): □ U.S. Civilian – International □ U.S. Civilian – Regional □ U.S. Civilian – Private Sector □ U.S. Military	Type of Airport (Foreign): □ Foreign – International □ Foreign – Regional □ Foreign – Private Sector □ Foreign – Military
□ Flight Operations POC and Location:	□ Airport Police/Security POC and Location: □ Jurisdiction:
□ U.S. DHS/TSA POC and Location:	□ Customs POC and Location:
□ Immigration/Passport/Visa POC and Location:	□ Fire Department POC and Location:

□ Crash and Fire Rescue POC and Location:	□ EMS POC and Location: □ Ambulance Response Time:
□ First-Aid Station POC and Location:	□ Ticket Counter of Airline POC and Location:
□ Security Checkpoint Location:	□ Rental Car Location and Contact Telephone:
□ Observation Deck Location:	□ Restaurant Locations:
□ VIP Lounge POC and Location:	□ VIP lounge Available: □ Yes □ No WIFI/Internet : □ Yes □ No
□ Barber Shop/Beauty Shop Location:	□ Foreign Currency Exchange Location:
□ Restroom Location(s):	□ News Stand/Gift Shop Location:

Airport Arrival Data

□ Type Aircraft:	□ Call Sign:	□ Tail Number:
□ Meet and Greet POC:		□ Telephone:

□ Describe Arrival Ceremony (if applicable):

Aircraft Requirements: □ Staircase □ Ramp/Jetway
□ Conveyor Belt (Luggage)
□ Shuttle
□ Other (Describe):

□ Luggage/Baggage POC and Location:	□ Luggage/Baggage Procedures:

Customs Clearance Procedures:

□ None/NA

□ Customs Officials Will Board Aircraft For a Briefing and/or Inspection

□ Customs Officials will Meet in Terminal Area

□ Firearms and Ammunition Clearance Procedures

□ Additional Procedures (describe):

Passport/Visa Clearance Procedures:

□ None/NA

□ Passports Will Be Collected and Provided to POC for Processing

□ Principal and Detail Must Pass Through Passport Control

□ Additional Procedures (describe):

□ Description of Motorcade Staging Area (Attach Photo and/or Sketch): Accessible to TARMAC: □ Yes □ No

Media Coverage:	Media Location(s):
□ Unknown	□ Throughout airport
□ Yes (describe):	□ Motorcade curbside
□ No	□ Designated press conference area
	□ Other
	□ Unknown

□ Media POC:	□ Telephone:

Media Credential Verification: □ Yes – By Venue Sponsor □ Yes – By Principal's Staff □ Yes – By Protection Detail □ No □ NA	**Media Representation:** □ National News (TV/radio) □ International News Organizations □ Print Media □ Video/Still Photography □ Armed Forces TV/Radio

On-Site Police/Security:
□ No
□ Yes (Uniform) Qty. on Duty: __
□ Yes (Plain Clothes)
Qty. on Duty: __
□ Unknown
	On-Site Police/Security Personnel:
	Armed: □ Yes □ No
	Arrest Authority: □ Yes □ No
	First-Aid/CPR Trained:
	  □ Yes □ No
	Access Master Keys/Card:
	  □ Yes □ No
	Access Elevator System:
	  □ Yes □ No
	English-Speaking □ Yes □ No

Fire Alarm System: Local Alarms Only: □ Yes □ No Site Security Auto Alert: □ Yes □ No Fire Dept Auto Alert: □ Yes □ No Unknown □ During Activation: □ Strobe □ Siren □ Horn □ Other	**Sprinkler System:** Water: □ Yes □ No Foam/Chemical: □ Yes □ No HALON: □ Yes □ No Unknown □
□ Location of Fire Extinguishers:	
□ Location of Fire Alarm Pull Stations:	

□ Location of Onsite Medical Equipment/AED:

Closed-Circuit Video/Camera: □ No □ Yes − Recorded □ Yes − Not Recorded	□ Location of Monitors and Cameras (Attach Photo and/or Sketch):

□ Length of Time that Camera Tapes are Maintained:

Role of Airport Facility Security Personnel During Principal Stay:

□ None

□ Elevator Access Control

□ Roving Foot Patrol

□ Roving Automobile Patrol

□ Coordination with Law Enforcement

□Traffic/Parking/Motorcade Security

□ Security Checkpoints: (list locations)

□ Instructions to Detail/Agents (Arrival):

Airport Departure Data

□ Type Aircraft:	□ Call Sign:	□ Tail Number:

□ Meet and Greet POC:	□ Telephone:

□ Describe Departure Ceremony (if applicable):

Aircraft Requirements: □ Staircase □ Ramp/Jetway

□ Conveyor Belt (Luggage)

□ Shuttle □ Other (describe):

Luggage/Baggage Sweep Before Departure: □ Yes □ No		
□ Location of Luggage/Baggage Sweep:		
□ K-9	□ POC:	□ Telephone:
□ X-Ray	□ POC:	□ Telephone:
□ Magnetometer	□ POC:	□ Telephone:
□ Other:	□ POC:	□ Telephone:

Flying Armed: □ Yes □ No   Procedures:
Customs Clearance Procedures: □ None/NA □ Customs Officials Will Board Aircraft for a Briefing and/or Inspection □ Customs Officials Will Meet in Terminal Area □ Additional Procedures (describe):
Passport/Visa Clearance Procedures: □ None/NA □ Passports Will be Collected and Provided to POC for Processing □ Principal and Detail Must Pass Through Passport Control □ Additional Procedures:
□ Description of Motorcade Staging Area (Attach Photo and/or Sketch): Accessible to TARMAC: □ Yes □ No

Media Coverage: ☐ Unknown ☐ Yes (describe): ☐ No	**Media Location(s):** ☐ Throughout airport ☐ Motorcade curbside ☐ Designated press conference area ☐ Other ☐ Unknown
☐ Media POC:	☐ Telephone:
☐ Media Credential Verification: ☐ Yes – By venue sponsor ☐ Yes – By Principal's staff ☐ Yes – By protection detail ☐ No ☐ NA	☐ Media Representation: ☐ National News (TV/radio) ☐ International News Organizations ☐ Print Media ☐ Video/Still Photography ☐ Armed Forces TV/Radio
On-Site Police/Security: ☐ No ☐ Yes (Uniform) Qty. on Duty: __ ☐ Yes (Plain Clothes) Qty. on Duty:__ ☐ Unknown	**On-Site Police/Security Personnel:** Armed: ☐ Yes ☐ No Arrest Authority: ☐ Yes ☐ No First-Aid/CPR Trained: ☐ Yes ☐ No Access Master Keys/Card: ☐ Yes ☐ No Access Elevator System: ☐ Yes ☐ No English-Speaking ☐ Yes ☐ No

Fire Alarm System:	Sprinkler System:
Local Alarms Only: □ Yes □ No	Water: □ Yes □ No
Site Security Auto Alert:	Foam/Chemical: □ Yes □ No
□ Yes □ No	HALON: □ Yes □ No
Fire Dept Auto Alert: □ Yes □ No	Unknown □
Unknown □	
During Activation:	
□ Strobe	
□ Siren	
□ Horn	
□ Other	

□ Location of Fire Extinguishers:

□ Location of Fire Alarm Pull Stations:

□ Location of Medical Equipment/AED:

Closed-Circuit Video/Camera:	□ Location of Monitors and Cameras
□ No	(attach photo and/or sketch):
□ Yes – Recorded	
□ Yes – Not Recorded	

□ Length of Time That Camera Tapes are Maintained:

Role of Airport Facility Security Personnel During Principal Stay:
□ None
□ Elevator Access Control
□ Roving Foot Patrol
□ Roving Automobile Patrol
□ Coordination with Law Enforcement
□Traffic/Parking/Motorcade Security
□ Security Checkpoints: (List Locations)

□ Instructions to Detail/Agents (Departure):

HOTEL SURVEY

Pre-Advance Phase: Use the below table to plan considerations for a hotel survey.

Any overnight travel of the Principal and the executive protection detail will most likely require lodging in a hotel. A hotel will need to be surveyed thoroughly as extensive administrative, logistical, and security factors must be considered. A hotel survey is unique in itself in that the Principal may not only work from the hotel, but may also participate in leisure activities, including dining, physical training, socializing, etc. The advance agent and advance team members will need to consider all of the needs of the Principal as it relates to his/her itinerary.

Advance Phase: Upon the physical occupation of the hotel, additional data may be discovered that was not considered during the pre-advance phase. Use the table to validate data previously collected or to modify the new data discovered during the advance phase.

HOTEL SURVEY
□ Date Survey Was Conducted: □ Time of Day: □ Advance Agent:
□ Name of Venue:

□ Street Address:		
□ City:	□ State/Country (OCONUS):	□ Zip Code:
□ Map of Region:	□ Blueprint/Floorplan:	
□ Description of Venue (attach photo and/or sketch):		
□ Scenario of Venue (What Will Take Place?):		

□ Planned Arrival Date:	□ Planned Arrival Time:	□ Planned Departure Date:	□ Planned Departure Time:

□ Weather Prediction (Date of Event):
□ Primary Point of Contact (POC)/Meet-and-Greet Contact:

□ Primary Point of Contact (POC)/□ Meet-and-Greet Contact Information:	□ Telephone: □ Alternate Telephone: □ Email:
□ Hotel Reservations (If Applicable):	
□ Airline Reservations (If Applicable):	

Type of Hotel: □ Public □ Private Residence □ U.S. Military Distinguished Visitor Quarters □ Foreign Military Distinguished Visitor Quarters □ Other	Will Hotel Accept a Federal Tax Exempt Letter? □ Yes □ No	Will Hotel Accept Credit Cards? □ Yes □ No Type:
List of Personnel Whom are Lodging Above/Below/Next to Principal: □ Yes □ No □ POC:	List of Hotel Staff Whom are Providing Personal Services to Principal: □ Yes □ No	
Room Rate: □ Single: □ Suite: Breakfast Included: □ Yes □ No	□ Foreign Currency Exchange Rate: $1.00 = _____ □ Gratuity Recommendations:	
□ Business Center Hours: Location:	□ Currency Exchange Hours: Location:	□ Laundry/Dry Cleaning Hours: Location:
□ Fitness Center Hours: Location:	□ Swimming Pool Hours: Location:	□ Restaurant Hours: Location:
□ Sauna Hours: Location:	□ Masseuse: Hours: Location:	□ Tennis Courts: Hours: Location:
□ Golf Course: Hours: Location:	□ Beverage Bar: Hours: Location:	□ Jogging/Hiking Trails Location:
□ Porter/Luggage Service:	□ Check-In Time: □ Check-Out Time:	□ Room Service □ Hours:

□ Safe Deposit Box Location:	□ Wire Service:	□ Notary Public:
□ Barber/Beauty Shop Location:	□ News Stand/Gift Shop Hours: Location:	□ Cable Television/Movie Capabilities:

Internet Access:

□ In Room – Access Code/Password:

□ Business Center – Access Code/Password:

□ None

□ Other Local Site Location:

Can Furniture be Moved and/or Exchanged at Room Being Used as a Command Post? □ Yes   □ No Additional Fee/Charges:

Electrical Current (OCONUS)

□ 110V   Converters Required: □ Yes □ No

□ 220V

□ Other

□ Additional Amenities:

English Spoken at Hotel: □ Yes □ No	Interpreter on Duty/Available □ Yes □ No
□ General Manager/POC:	□ Telephone:
□ Alternate POC:	□ Telephone:
Building Engineer POC: 24 Hour on Duty: □ Yes □ No Hrs:	Telephone:

□ Procedures for Elevator Maintenance Issues/Inspections: □ Procedures for HVAC Maintenance Issues: Access to HVAC: □ Yes □ No Location: Access to Electrical Box: □ Yes □ No Location: Access to Roof: □ Yes □ No Location:	

Access Control of Elevators: All Floors: □ Yes □ No Some Floors: □ Yes □ No None □	Access Control of Garage: Attendant: □ Yes □ No Key/Card: □ Yes □ No None □
Access Control of Garage: Attendant: □ Yes □ No Key/Card: □ Yes □ No None □	Access Control of Roof: Key/Card: □ Yes □ No Location of Access:
□ Maitre D' POC:	□ Telephone:
□ Bell Captain POC:	□ Telephone:
□ Security POC:	□ Telephone:
□ Law Enforcement POC:	□ Telephone:
□ Fire Department POC:	□ Telephone:
□ Hospital POC:	□ Telephone:

□ Nearest Hospital Name and Street Address:

□ City:	□ State:	□ Zip Code:

On-Site Police/Security: □ No □ Yes (Uniform) Qty. on Duty: __ □ Yes (Plain Clothes) Qty. on Duty: __ □ Unknown	On-Site Police/Security Personnel: Armed: □ Yes □ No Arrest Authority: □ Yes □ No First-Aid/CPR Trained: □ Yes □ No Access Master Keys/Card: □ Yes □ No Access Elevator System: □ Yes □ No English-Speaking □ Yes □ No

□ Hotel Events That May Impact Safety and/or Security of Principal:

□ Local Area Events/Known Criminal /Terrorist Activities That May Impact Safety and/or Security of Principal:

□ Other Executive Protection Details That Will Be Present During Principal's Itinerary: □ POCs and Contact Information of Other Details:

Fire Alarm System: Local Alarms Only: □ Yes □ No Site Security Auto Alert: □ Yes □ No Fire Dept Auto Alert: □ Yes □ No Unknown □ During Activation: □ Strobe □ Siren □ Horn □ Other	Sprinkler System: Water: □ Yes □ No Foam/Chemical: □ Yes □ No HALON: □ Yes □ No Unknown □

□ Location of Fire Extinguishers:

□ Location of Fire Alarm Pull Stations:

□ Highest Floor that a Fire Ladder Truck and/or Equipment Can Reach:

□ Location of Onsite Medical Equipment/AEDs:

Closed-Circuit Video/Camera: □ No □ Yes – Recorded □ Yes – Not Recorded	□ Location of Monitors and Cameras: (attach photo and/or sketch)

□ Length of Time that Camera Tapes are Maintained:

Role of Hotel Security Personnel During Principal Stay:

□ None

□ Elevator Access Control

□ Roving Foot Patrol

□ Roving Automobile Patrol

□ Coordination with Law Enforcement

□Traffic/Parking/Motorcade Security

□ Security Checkpoints: (list locations)

Use the below as a checklist for surveying the Principal Suite/Room

□ Suite Number:	Safe □ Yes □ No Code:	□ Telephone: Number:
□ Door and Window Locks:	□ Smoke Detectors:	□ Sprinkler System:
□ Climate Control:	□ Lighting:	□ Television/Movies:

□ Bathroom and Shower:	□ Bottled Water:	□ Emergency Exits:

□ Principal Suite Security Sweep:		

□ K-9	□ POC:	□ Telephone:
□ X-Ray	□ POC:	□ Telephone:
□ Magnetometer	□ POC:	□ Telephone:
□ Explosive Ordnance Disposal:	□ POC:	□ Telephone:
□ Technical	□ POC:	□ Telephone:
□ Other:	□ POC:	□ Telephone:

ARRIVAL

□ Description of Motorcade Staging Area (Attach Photo and/or Sketch):   □ Location of Stash Car:
□ Arrival Location: (attach photo and/or sketch):
□ Person to Greet Principal/Official Party:
□ Location of Greeter:
Security Checkpoint at Entrance: □ Yes – Type □ Magnetometer □ Hand Screen □ Invitation/Pass □ Other: □ No

Is Principal Authorized to Bypass Security Checkpoint(s)?	
□ Yes – Principal Only □ Yes – Principal and Spouse □ Yes – Principal and Other: □ No:	

Media Coverage:	Media Location(s):
□ Unknown □ Yes (describe): □ No	□ Throughout Venue □ Motorcade Curbside □ Designated Press Conference Area □ Other □ Unknown
□ Media POC:	□ Telephone:

Media Credential Verification:	Media Representation:
□ Yes – By Venue Sponsor □ Yes – By Principal's Staff □ Yes – By Protection Detail □ No □ NA	□ National News (TV/radio) □ International News Organizations □ Print Media □ Video/Still Photography □ Armed Forces TV/Radio

□ Nearest Restroom Location On Entry:	

Location of Principal's Room Key(s):	Date/Time That Room Keys Will Be Available for Detail:
□ Detail Command Post □ Embassy Control Room □ Front Desk Registration □ Other	Location of Spare Keys: □ Detail Command Post □ AIC/SL

□ Location of Elevators:	□ Location of Escalators:	□ Location of Stairwells: □ Number of Flights:
Elevator Lockdown Procedures: □ Yes - Attendant □ Yes – Key/Control Panel □ No □ NA	□ Capacity of Elevator: □ Maximum Weight: □ Maximum Occupants:	□ Last Inspection Date of Elevator:
□ Location of Elevator For Baggage:	□ Baggage Unloading Area:	□ Number of Baggage

□ Walking Route From Arrival Point to Principal's Room:

□ Location and Description of Safe Haven: □ Route from Principal's Room to Safe Haven:

□ Principal's Room Number: □ Floor:	Will Elevators Be Used? □ Yes □ No – Stairwells Will Be Used □ NA

□ Post Assignments (Arrival): □ Directions to Detail/Agents:

DEPARTURE

□ Description of Motorcade Staging Area (Attach Photo and/or Sketch): □ Location of Stash Car:

□ Departure Location: (attach photo and/or sketch):
□ Person to Greet Principal on Send-Off Party:
□ Location of Send-Off Party:

Media Coverage:	Media Location(s):
□ Unknown	□ Throughout Venue
□ Yes (describe):	□ Motorcade Curbside
□ No	□ Designated Press Conference Area
	□ Other
	□ Unknown
□ Media POC:	□ Telephone:
Media Credential Verification:	Media Representation:
□ Yes – By Venue Sponsor	□ National News (TV/radio)
□ Yes – By Principal's Staff	□ International News Organizations
□ Yes – By Protection Detail	□ Print Media
□ No	□ Video/Still Photography
□ NA	□ Armed Forces TV/Radio

□ Date and Time of Official Party Baggage Disembark:
Location of Baggage:
□ Delivered to Command Post
□ Delivered to Embassy Control Room
□ Other:

Luggage Sweeps		
□ K-9	□ POC:	□ Telephone:
□ X-Ray	□ POC:	□ Telephone:
□ Magnetometer	□ POC:	□ Telephone:
□ Explosive Ordnance Disposal:	□ POC:	□ Telephone:
□ Other:	POC:	Telephone:
□ Post Assignments (Departure):		
□ Directions to Detail/Agents:		

RESTAURANT SURVEY

Pre-Advance Phase: Use the below table to record data for a restaurant survey.

Restaurants pose unique logistical and security considerations in themselves as the executive protection detail must weigh the security considerations of the venue against the potential of negatively impacting the general operations of the restaurant and its accessibility to the public.

During the pre-advance phase, the executive protection detail may attempt to coordinate a private dining arrangement for the Principal, but this may not always be possible. A public setting may be the only option. Of course, many factors will come into play including the profile of the venue, the threat level, the geographic location, and many other environmental factors. Regardless, the restaurant venue may pose significant challenges to the executive protection detail, and comprehensive administrative, logistical, and security factors must be considered.

Advance Phase: The data collected during the pre-advance phase will be validated and/or modified during the physical occupation of restaurant during the advance phase. Update the table to reflect any new data that was not previously considered.

RESTAURANT SURVEY

☐ Date Survey Was Conducted:

☐ Time of Day:

☐ Advance Agent:

☐ Name of Venue:

☐ Street Address:

☐ City:	☐ State/Country (OCONUS):	☐ Zip Code:

☐ Map of Region:	☐ Blue Print/Floor Plan:

☐ Word Description of Venue (Attach Photo and/or Sketch):

☐ Scenario of Venue (What Will Take Place?):

☐ Planned Arrival Date:	☐ Planned Arrival Time:	☐ Planned Departure Date:	☐ Planned Departure Time:

☐ Weather Prediction (Date of Event):

☐ Restaurant Manager:	☐ Telephone:
	☐ Alternate Telephone:
	☐ Email:

☐ Maitre D':	☐ Telephone:
	☐ Alternate Telephone:
	☐ Email:

□ Type of Cuisine Served:	□ Copy of Menu: □ Yes □ No
	□ Copy of Wine List: □ Yes □ No

□ Reservations Required: □ Yes □ No

□ Date of Last Health Inspection:

□ Alcohol Service: □ Yes □ No

□ Smoking Authorized: □ Yes □ No Location:

□ Private Rooms: □ Yes □ No Location:

□ Dress Code:

□ Seating Capacity:

□ Method of Payment: □ Cash □ Credit Card □ Check

English Spoken at Restaurant:	Interpreter on Duty/Available
□ Yes □ No	□ Yes □ No

□ Events That May Impact Safety and/or Security of Principal:

□ Local Area Events/Known Criminal /Terrorist Activities That May Impact Safety and/or Security of Principal:

□ Other Executive Protection Details That Will Be Present During Principal's Itinerary:

□ POCs and Contact Information of Other Details:

Fire Alarm System:	Sprinkler System:
Local Alarms Only: □ Yes □ No	Water: □ Yes □ No
Site Security Auto Alert: □ Yes □ No	Foam/Chemical: □ Yes □ No
Fire Dept Auto Alert: □ Yes □ No	HALON: □ Yes □ No
Unknown □	Unknown □
During Activation:	
□ Strobe	
□ Siren	
□ Horn	
□ Other	

□ Location of Fire Extinguishers:

□ Location of Fire Alarm Pull Stations:

□ Location of Medical Equipment/AEDs:

Closed-Circuit Video/Camera:	□ Location of Monitors and Cameras:
□ No	(attach photo and/or sketch)
□ Yes – Recorded	
□ Yes – Not Recorded	

□ Length of Time that Camera Tapes are Maintained:

ARRIVAL

□ Description of Motorcade Staging Area (Attach Photo and/or Sketch):
□ Location of Stash Car:

□ Arrival Location(s): (Attach Photo and/or Sketch):

□ Person to Greet Principal/Official Party:

□ Location of Greeter:

Media Coverage:

□ Unknown

□ Yes (describe):

□ No

Details:

□ Media POC:	□ Telephone:

□ Restroom Location(s):

□ Walking Route From Arrival Point:

□ Location and Description of Safe Haven:

□ Route from Principal's Table/Seat to Safe Haven:

□ Locations of Ingress/Egress:

□ Post Assignments (Arrival):

□ Directions to Detail/Agents:

DEPARTURE

□ Description of Motorcade Staging Area (Attach Photo and/or Sketch):

□ Location of Stash Car:

□ Departure Location(s): (Attach Photo and/or Sketch):

□ Person to Greet Principal on Send-Off Party:

☐ Location of Send-Off Party:

Media Coverage:
☐ Unknown
☐ Yes (describe):
☐ No
Details:

☐ Media POC:	☐ Telephone:

☐ Walking Route to Departure Point:

☐ Location and Description of Safe Haven:
☐ Route from Principal's Table/Seat to Safe Haven:

☐ Locations of Ingress/Egress:

☐ Post Assignments (Arrival):

☐ Directions to Detail/Agents:

PRIVATE RESIDENCE SURVEY

Pre-Advance Phase: Use the below table to record data for the survey of a private residence. It is advised to use the hotel survey table and then supplement the data by also including the data of this table.

Private residences are unique in that no two are alike. The floor plan, interior layout, furniture, personal effects, exterior spaces, yard, green space, etc. serve to make each venue unique.

Advance Phase: Data that was collected during the pre-advance phase will be validated and/or modified upon the physical occupation and survey of the private residence.

PRIVATE RESIDENCE SURVEY		
□ Date Survey Was Conducted: □ Time of Day: □ Advance Agent:		
□ Name of Venue:		
□ Street Address:		
□ City:	□ State/Country (OCONUS):	□ Zip Code:

Map of Region:	Blue Print/Floor Plan:

□ Word description of Venue (Attach Photo and/or Sketch):

□ Scenario of Venue (What Will Take Place?):

□ Planned Arrival Date:	□ Planned Arrival Time:	□ Planned Departure Date:	□ Planned Departure Time:

□ Weather Prediction (Date of Event):

□ Primary Point of Contact (POC)/Meet-and-Greet Contact:

□ Determine Principal's Room/Quarters:

□ Determine Safe Haven:

□ Determine Location and Details of Temporary Command Post:

□ Obtain Guest Roster:

□ Obtain Roster of Personnel On Property (During Itinerary):

□ Determine Procedures for Handling Caterers, Entertainers, etc.

□ Determine Food Arrangements for Principal and Detail:

□ Acquire Spare Keys to Principal's Room (If Applicable):

□ Determine Telephone and Radio Communications Procedures:

□ Determine Media Considerations (If Applicable):

Determine On-Site Security Considerations:
☐ Fencing:
☐ Gates:
☐ Ingress/Egress Routes:
☐ Security Cameras:
☐ Alarms:
☐ Location of Motorcade Arrival/Departure/Parking/Stash Car:
☐ Determine Location and Access to Firearms and Ammunition:
☐ Determine Plan for Handling Unexpected Visitors/Guests:
☐ Dangerous Pets/Exotic Animals:
☐ Determine Plan for Handling Suspicious Mail and/or Packages:
☐ Inquire With Owner Regarding Criminal Activity/Suspicious Incidents:
☐ Interview/Screen Adjacent Neighbors:
Determine Location and Considerations For: ☐ Electrical Circuit Box: ☐ Heating/Ventilation/Air Conditioning: ☐ Property Lines and Floor Plan:
☐ Post Assignments:
☐ Directions to Detail/Agents:

GENERIC BUILDING SURVEY

Pre-Advance Phase: Use the below table to record data for the survey of a building or facility that is not described in the existing tables of this guide.

Any building or facility that the Principal may frequent during his/her itinerary should be surveyed, if at all possible. The table below contains elements from other tables; however, it also contains some elements that are unique to a generic building survey.

Advance Phase: Data collected during the pre-advance phase will be validated and/or modified during the advance phase. Additional data that was discovered during the physical survey of the building will be added to the below table.

GENERIC BUILDING SURVEY		
□ Date Survey Was Conducted: □ Time of Day: □ Advance Agent:		
□ Street Address:		
□ City:	□ State/Country (OCONUS):	□ Zip Code:
□ Map of Region:		□ Blue Print/Floor Plan:

□ Word description of Venue (Attach Photo and/or Sketch):			
□ Scenario of Venue (What Will Take Place?):			
□ Planned Arrival Date:	□ Planned Arrival Time:	□ Planned Departure Date:	□ Planned Departure Time:
□ Weather Prediction (Date of Event):			
□ Primary Point of Contact (POC)/Meet-and-Greet Contact Information:		□ Telephone: □ Alternate Telephone: □ Email:	
□ Type of Facility:		□ Number of Floors:	
□ Number of Employees:		□ Number of Tenants:	
Internet Access: □ Yes □ No □ Describe Procedures:			
Electrical Current (OCONUS) □ 110V Converters Required: □ Yes □ No □ 220V □ Other			
English Spoken By Staff: □ Yes □ No		Interpreter on Duty/Available □ Yes □ No	
Primary POC:		Telephone:	
Alternate POC:		Telephone:	

□ Procedures for Elevator Maintenance Issues/Inspections: □ Procedures for HVAC Maintenance Issues: Access to HVAC: □ Yes □ No Location: Access to Electrical Box: □ Yes □ No Location: Access to Roof: □ Yes □ No Location:	
Access Control of Elevators: All Floors: □ Yes □ No Some Floors: □ Yes □ No None □	Access Control of Garage: Attendant: □ Yes □ No Key/Card: □ Yes □ No None □
Access Control of Garage: Attendant: □ Yes □ No Key/Card: □ Yes □ No None □	Access Control of Roof: Key/Card: □ Yes □ No Location of Access:
□ Security POC:	□ Telephone:
□ Law Enforcement POC:	□ Telephone:
□ Fire Department POC:	□ Telephone:
□ Hospital POC:	□ Telephone:
□ Nearest Hospital Name and Street Address:	
□ City: □ State:	□ Zip Code:

On-Site Police/Security:
□ No
□ Yes (Uniform) Qty. on Duty: __
□ Yes (Plain Clothes) Qty. on Duty: __
□ Unknown
	On-Site Police/Security Personnel:
	Armed: □ Yes □ No
	Arrest Authority: □ Yes □ No
	First-Aid/CPR Trained:
	  □ Yes □ No
	Access Master Keys/Card:
	  □ Yes □ No
	Access Elevator System:
	  □ Yes □ No
	English-Speaking □ Yes □ No

□ Facility Events That May Impact Safety and/or Security of Principal:

□ Local Area Events/Known Criminal /Terrorist Activities That May Impact Safety and/or Security of Principal:

□ Other Executive Protection Details That Will Be Present During Principal's Itinerary: □ POCs and Contact Information of Other Details:

Fire Alarm System: Local Alarms Only: □ Yes □ No Site Security Auto Alert: □ Yes □ No Fire Dept Auto Alert: □ Yes □ No Unknown □ During Activation: □ Strobe □ Siren □ Horn □ Other	Sprinkler System: Water: □ Yes □ No Foam/Chemical: □ Yes □ No HALON: □ Yes □ No Unknown □

□ Location of Fire Extinguishers:

□ Location of Fire Alarm Pull Stations:

□ Highest Floor that a Fire Ladder Truck and/or Equipment Can Reach:

□ Location of Medical Equipment/AEDs:

Closed-Circuit Video/Camera: □ No □ Yes – Recorded □ Yes – Not Recorded	□ Location of Monitors and Cameras: (attach photo and/or sketch)

□ Length of Time that Camera Tapes are Maintained:

Role of Facility Security Personnel During Principal Stay: □ None □ Elevator Access Control □ Roving Foot Patrol □ Roving Automobile Patrol □ Coordination with Law Enforcement □Traffic/Parking/Motorcade Security □ Security Checkpoints(list locations):

Nearest Restroom Location On Entry:

Location of Elevators:	Location of Escalators:	Location of Stairwells: Number of Flights:

Elevator Lockdown Procedures: □ Yes - Attendant □ Yes – Key/Control Panel □ No □ NA	Capacity of Elevator: Maximum Weight: Maximum Occupants:	Last Inspection Date of Elevator:

Walking Route From Arrival Point to Principal's Venue:

Location and Description of Safe Haven: Route from Principal's Venue to Safe Haven:

Principal's Room Number: Floor:	Will Elevators Be Used? □ Yes □ No – Stairwells Will Be Used □ NA

Post Assignments:

Directions to Detail/Agents:

INTERNATIONAL TRAVEL

The mission and professional profile of an executive protection detail's Principal may dictate that his/her role requires international travel from the home nation to a foreign nation. Of course, like any other executive protection operation, the protection detail will need to travel with the Principal in order to provide for the logistical and security requirements of the Principal's travel.

International executive protection operations can vary significantly from domestic operations that are conducted in the executive protection detail's home nation. The laws, rules, and regulations may be vastly different in the foreign region, and this may change the mission profile and standard operating procedures of the executive protection detail.

It is critical that the advance agent and advance team understand the administrative, logistical, security, and legal requirements of the nation that will be traveled. Extensive research and planning will be required in order to ensure that no detail has been left untouched.

The below table will serve as a general guideline in the conduct of advance planning for international travel. The advance agent and his/her team may add additional contents to the table as they determine a need that may not be currently displayed in the table. Complete one table for each foreign nation on the Principal's itinerary.

Additionally, use the other tables of this guide to supplement the international travel considerations. For example, if the Principal will be staying at a hotel through the course of his/her international travel and itinerary, a hotel survey will be conducted.

INTERNATIONAL TRAVEL CONSIDERATIONS

□ Date Table Was Completed:

□ Advance Agent:

□ Principal's Itinerary and Schedules:

□ Principal's Participating:

□ Date(s) of Principal's Travel:

□ Official Business: □ Yes □ No	□ Personal/Pleasure: □ Yes □ No

□ Continent:	□ Nation:	□ City:
□ Time Zone:	□ Difference in Time (from local time): □ Ahead □ Behind □ Number of Hours:	□ Specific Destination/Address on Principal's Itinerary: □ Lat/Lon Coordinates:
Terrain: □ Plains □ Dessert □ Mountain □ Jungle □ Other:	Climate: □ Tropical □ Dry □ Temperate □ Cold □ Polar	□ Altitude at Principal's Venue:

□ Natural Resources:

□ Primary Export Goods:

☐ Primary Import Goods:

☐ English Spoken as the Primary Language: ☐ Yes ☐ No
Primary Language(s):

☐ Religion(s):
☐ Religious Rituals/Customs/Holidays:

☐ Local Customs:

☐ Special Customs and Protocol Sensitivities *(i.e. women's heads covered, alcohol restrictions, etc.):*

☐ Political Climate and Current Events:

☐ Type of Government:

☐ Nation's Person in Power:

☐ Nation's Allies:

☐ Nation's Enemies:

☐ Education/School and University System:

☐ Passport Requirements for Principal, Staff, and EP Detail:

☐ Passport Cover (Generic):

☐ Global Entry Application from U.S. Customs and Border Protection (if applicable):

□ Visa and Customs Requirements:

□ Gift Exchange Customs and Protocols:
□ Recommended Value of Gifts:

□ Type of Currency:	□ Monetary Exchange: $1.00 = ____

□ Coordinate with Mobile Telephone Carrier for International Plans:

□ Acquire Mobile Telephone SIM Card (if applicable):

□ Assign SIM Cards to EP Agent Mobile Telephones (If applicable):

□ Coordinate Radio Communication Requirements (Frequencies, Repeaters, etc.):

□ Coordinate Additional Communication Requirements:

Security Considerations

□ Principal and EP Detail Attendance of U.S. Department of State Security Overseas Seminar (SOS)
(NOTE: Required for U.S. Federal Government Personnel, if deployed more than 30 days):

□ Country Briefing from U.S. Department of State:

□ Research Travel.State.Gov Website:

□ Research USEmbassy.Gov Website:

□ Coordinate with U.S. Embassy and Consulates (if applicable):

□ Firearm Regulations/Restrictions:

□ Firearm Carry Protocols:
Concealed: □ Yes □ No
Open Carry: □ Yes □ No

□ Firearm Checkpoint Procedures:

□ Firearms/Weapons/Ammunition/Pyrotechnics Authorized:

□ Firearms/Weapons/Ammunition/Pyrotechnics Unauthorized:

□ U.S. Citizen Evacuation Protocols and Requirements (U.S. Embassy):

□ Coordinate Motorcade and Driver Considerations:

□ Proprietary/In-House Travel Security Program (if applicable):

□ Route and Venue Surveys (use tables in this guide):

□ Known Terrorist Groups and Criminal Organizations:

□ Law Enforcement and Security Points of Contact:

□ Fire Service Points of Contact:

Health and Medical Considerations

□ Immunizations Required Prior to Departure from Home Nation:

□ Immunizations Required Upon Entering Nation/Port of Entry (POE):

□ Known Regional Diseases and/or Health Concerns:

□ Survey Medical Facilities:

□ MEDEVAC Protocols and Procedures:

ADVANCE PHASE

The Advance Planning Phase can best be defined as the actual physical occupation and survey of the route(s) and venue survey(s) that are included in the Principal's itinerary.

All of the planning, liaison, and coordination conducted during the pre-advance phase will now be validated and/or modified upon the advance agent and advance team members physically occupying the routes and venues.

The proper way to execute the advance phase is to use the Principal's itinerary in conjunction with the tables that were completed during the pre-advance phase. The advance team will conduct a reconnaissance of the proposed routes, including a primary route and at least one alternate route to each venue.

Additionally, each venue in the Principal's itinerary will be surveyed by speaking with onsite stakeholders and key points of contact, walking the venue, viewing points of ingress and egress, physically inspecting logistical and security features, and validating and/or modifying other data points.

All of the data that was recorded in the pre-advance phase tables will be validated and/or modified as each route and venue survey is conducted. Essentially, the table is used as a checklist by the advance agent and advance team to ensure that information from the pre-advance phase is still current or needs updating and modification.

Ultimately, once the data is validated and/or modified and updated, the advance phase tables will be presented to the executive protection detail's leadership for the purpose of developing the Executive Protection Operation Plan.

EXECUTIVE PROTECTION OPERATIONAL PLANNING PHASE

The Executive Protection Operational Plan is defined as the tactics, techniques, and procedures (TTPs) that the executive protection detail will utilize during the conduct of the executive protection operation.

It serves to illustrate the administrative, logistical, legal, and security considerations and provide a written format for the execution of the executive protection operation.

The plan subscribes to a reverse engineering approach that commences with the Principal's Itinerary. Everything that will take place in order to support the itinerary is detailed in the operational plan. Essentially, all of the data that was collected during the Pre-Advance Phase and the Advance Phase will ultimately become elements of the executive protection operational plan.

Every executive protection detail should have a standard operating procedure (SOP) for the development and delivery of an operational plan. This will provide a consistent format and will serve to be a great asset in terms of time management and consistency in communications among executive protection detail agents.

Upon the completion of all advance operations, the advance agent and advance team members will provide the data to the leadership of the executive protection detail. The detail's leadership will then determine the agents whom will develop and finalize the operational plan.

Oftentimes, the agents whom performed the advance work will also prepare the operational plan as they are the agents whom are familiar with the finite administrative, legal, logistical, and security details and considerations. It only makes sense that these personnel, at minimum, assist in the plan's development and delivery.

5-Paragraph Order: The Executive Protection Operational Plan that is illustrated in this guide subscribes to the U.S. Department of Defense (DOD) 5-paragraph operational order model.

Note: Organizations may, of course, select any model that serves their requirements. The main point of emphasis is that the operational plan should be written utilizing a consistent model.

The DOD model uses five main paragraphs to illustrate the plan. The easiest way to remember the main paragraphs is to use the acronym: SMEAC.

1. **Situation**
2. **Mission**
3. **Execution**
4. **Administration and Logistics**
5. **Command and Control**

1. **Situation:** Use this paragraph to orient the executive protection detail and describe the big picture of the Principal's itinerary. Information that may be included in this paragraph include:

   a. Principal(s) data
   b. Threat assessment (criminal/terrorist/known threats against Principal)
   c. Expected weather during the itinerary
   d. Additional expected dignitaries and security details
   e. Supporting organizations (police, fire, medical support, etc.)

2. **Mission:** Use this paragraph to provide the mission that is specific to the protection detail. This paragraph will include:

    a. Location (display maps, charts, photos, sketches, etc.)
    b. Dates of travel
    c. Dates/schedules of key venue events

3. **Execution:** This paragraph is typically the most lengthy and comprehensive paragraph of the plan. It will include the "who, what, when, where, how, and why" with respect to the detail's specific mission. This paragraph will include several sub paragraphs, including:

    a. Agent assignments and security posts
    b. Motorcade and driver instructions
    c. Route survey data
    d. Venue survey data
    e. Safe haven data and procedures
    f. Principal cover and evacuate procedures
    g. Emergency/contingency plans (worst case scenarios)

4. **Administration and Logistics:** This paragraph will provide considerations for administrative details as well as considerations for food, water, equipment, etc. This paragraph will illustrate the following:

    a. Dress code for Principal and agents
    b. Travel accommodations/reservations
    c. Equipment for the Principal
    d. Firearms/weapons and ammunition requirements
    e. Equipment for each agent
    f. Mission-specific detail equipment
    g. Command post equipment
    h. Motorcade equipment
    i. Plan for feeding agents
    j. Plan for rest and relief of agents and drivers

5. **Command and Signal:** This paragraph is used to provide information regarding command/control protocols as well as the means in which the detail will communicate with each other during the operation. Included in this paragraph:

    a. Location and organization of the command post
    b. Chain of command
    c. Communications security protocols
    d. Call signs
    e. Radio frequencies
    f. Cellular phone protocols
    g. Visual communications protocols
    h. Radios/communications equipment

Briefing the Plan: Once the executive protection operational plan has been completed, it will need to be briefed to all members of the executive protection detail.

Additionally, elements of the plan will also need to be briefed to the Principal(s), relevant family members and staff, and other stakeholders, as required. Briefing of these stakeholders should be separate from the agent briefing, and is normally conducted by the executive protection detail's leadership.

Organization standard operating procedures (SOPs) should dictate the protocols for briefing the plan; however, there are key factors that should be considered, if at all possible:

- Location should provide security, privacy, comfort, and adequate space for all members of the executive protection detail.

- Audio/visual media should be used to support the plan (i.e. PowerPoint, maps, charts, photographs, sketches, video, etc.).

- Briefing should be conducted by an agent with strong leadership and communication skills.

- Briefing should be delivered in a consistent format. Agents will grow accustomed to a consistent format and will be able to anticipate the order of delivery and key elements of the plan as it relates to them individually.

CONCLUSION

The essence of advance operations is risk analysis and the development of plans to mitigate the risks. All elements of the pre- advance phase, advance phase, and the executive protection operational plan support the mitigation of risks.

The ultimate success or failure of an executive protection operation will typically be attributed to the level of planning, attention to detail, and the coordination during advance operations.

Of course, there can never be an absolute guarantee that all administrative, logistical, legal and security considerations will be addressed by the advance agent and advance team members. Additionally, there can never be an absolute guarantee that the operation will be absent of a contingency, to include an embarrassing situation, an attack on the Principal, a medical emergency, or some other form of crisis.

When advance operations have been properly planned and executed, the Principal can be reasonably assured that the administrative and logistical requirements of his/her itinerary can be met, and that every foreseeable consideration has been addressed. Additionally, the Principal can rest assured that the security, safety, and reputation considerations of the operation have been addressed.